Contents

NOTHING CAN BE DONE, EVERYTHING IS POSSIBLE

BYRON KENNARD

Brick House Publishing Co., Inc.
Andover, Massachusetts

Published by:	**Brick House Publishing Co., Inc.** 34 Essex Street Andover, Massachusetts
Cover design:	Mike Fender
Typesetting:	Janet E. Lendall
Editor:	Linnea Ochs
Copy Prep:	Norma Wilton

Printed in the United States of America.

Library of Congress Cataloging in Publication Data

Kennard, Byron.
Nothing can be done, everything is possible.

1. United States — Social conditions — 1970–
2. Community organization — United States.
I. Title.

HN65.K44 973.92 81-21716
ISBN 0-931790-32-8 AACR2

Dedicated to my grandmother,
Dockie D. Bolin,
in gratitude for her love

All the truest sayings are paradoxical.

Lao Tse

Foreword

I occasionally have a fantasy. It's not an uncommon one; you may have had it too. I imagine that I am an all-powerful ruler who decrees the construction of a huge, life-size chessboard in the center of my country's principal stadium. All the pieces, the Knights on horseback, the pawns, and so on, are my personal friends and enemies. As thousands watch, I lock intellectual horns with my opponent, each of us ordering the living pieces to move where we tell them. The details of the game aren't really important. If I'm in a devilish mood, the human chesspersons in my fantasy draw knives and dispatch each other; if I'm feeling erotic, the climax of the game is a real "mate" before the assembled multitude. What <u>is</u> important is the power and intrigue and manipulation of real people through the life-emulating complexities of the chessboard.

Byron Kennard actually lives such a fantasy.

To Byron, the world is one continuous chess problem to be studied and contemplated, with hundreds of moves tried and pulled back and thousands of combinations analyzed, until just the right little nudge is decided upon - a judicious short letter here, a long, friendly phone call there, the perfectly planned intimate cocktail party, the brown-bag lunch with a startlingly original thinker from some far-off land.

But unlike my fantasy of a measly sixty-four-square chessboard with sixteen unimaginatively constrained pieces sliding around in two dimensions, Byron's real-life playing field contains thousands of uniquely shaped spaces arranged in three (or possibly even four) dimensions, uncounted numbers of pieces each with its own moves, rules that have never been compiled, and a time frame long enough to last a lifetime. If you've ever met Byron— if your name has ever shown up in some obscure footnote in a long-forgotten book that happened to catch his eye—you're in that chess game somewhere. You may be off on the fringes, awaiting action, or you may be front and center, one step from unexpectedly checkmating the king, but you are in there. For instance, I know I'm in there, merrily writing my first foreword to a book, smiling at my clever coup, wondering how I ever talked Byron into letting me pen these words, knowing somewhere deep down inside that I am a pawn or a bishop or a community-based innovator (one of his more recently invented pieces) humbly obeying a move preordained for me months ago by the master organizer himself.

Byron is continually reevaluating. He reevaluates his own life monthly (or more often if there is a crisis); he reevaluates his friends' lives for his purposes bimonthly; he reevaluates his friends' lives for their purposes about twice a year (it's an unsettling experience to have lunch with someone who takes out a sheaf of papers and says, "Well, I've been thinking about you since five o'clock this morning, and as I see it you have seven different options for the next year and a half."); and in the heat of an exciting campaign that he's involved with, he'll reevaluate all the participants hourly. Moreover, his reevaluations aren't the pathetic, gossipy excuses for thought that pass for brilliance in this tinsel town on the Potomac—they are page after notebook page of thoughts and references, strands from the newspaper, snippets from talk shows, citations from polls, quotes from past history, recollections of promises, all turned inside out and formulated into incisive, original syntheses that take your breath away.

Luckily for all of us, Byron is a mass of contradictions: an environmentalist who, I can promise, likes nothing less than going for a long hike in the woods, something he has undoubtedly never done; an advocate of appropriate technology who literally could not replace a blown fuse, much less understand the workings of a solar cell, despite his vice chairmanship of Sun Day; and now, more recently, a writer racked with periodic writer's block so bad that he once developed a rash on his hands that prevented him from either holding a pen or hitting the typewriter's keys. Contradictions are the spice of Byron's life and this book is filled with his ironic observations, from the title to the closing chapter. If you are hoping to find here happy little platitudes prancing around with easy answers and simplistic solutions, you'll be wrenchingly frustrated. But if you delight in the complexities and subtleties of life, in the quirks of interpersonal relationships, you'll have a ball.

In 1978, when we were working together on Sun Day, I as co-coordinator and he as board member and unofficial staff guru, we spent one afternoon talking about the progress the effort was making as May 3 approached. It had been a particularly difficult week, with frantic phone calls back and forth to Hollywood celebrities, Washington union officials, New York fat cats, Florida politicians, and many others. Everywhere we looked we saw fabulous opportunities marred by dismally complex realities. I was tense and frustrated by the hurdles and exclaimed, "Why is it so difficult to put together a successful event for such a worthwhile issue?"

"You've got it backwards," Byron explained. "Your job is to get past the hurdles. If you do, Sun Day will be a success on its own. You're not creating Sun Day—none of us are. The society itself is doing that. You are eliminating the roadblocks that normally prevent anything worthwhile from happening." Another contradiction, crystal clear and, of course, correct.

Being at a cocktail party with Byron is a real treat. Most Washington cocktail parties are brimful with three classes of people: the celebrities and near-celebs (members of congress, administration officials, heads of organizations, prominent journalists); the cause-pushers and the interest-defenders (lawyers, lobbyists, and public relations flacks); and the name-droppers (everyone else). Individuals in this first group stand in the corners of rooms surrounded by fawning admirers who generally keep handing them cards and pieces of paper. People in the second category race around, aggressively shaking hands while looking for deals to consummate and new victims to intimidate. Those in the last group stand near the food, drink in hand, looking past each other to peer about the room, pointing with their chins, eyes, or heads, and periodically screaming shrilly or bellowing manfully at the rare acquaintance low enough in the pecking order to actually be approached, hugged, or backslapped and brought into the nervous circle of food and gossip.

Then there's Byron. Nine times out of ten, when he is introduced at a cocktail party the reaction is, "So you're Byron Kennard! I've heard so much about you! I can't believe we're finally getting to meet!"

Ask these people exactly what it is they've heard about Byron and the enthusiasm turns to embarrassed vagueness. Isn't he the one who coined the phrase "small is beautiful?" Didn't he defeat the STT? Or was it DDT? Wasn't he Carter's campaign strategist for the 1976 Iowa caucuses? No, isn't he the psychic who predicted the Reagan shooting?

The fact is, no one really knows what Byron does, how or why he does it, what he lives on, or what he's after. People don't realize that the reason they've heard of him, the reason they take his phone calls even after instructing their secretaries to hold everything but the emergencies, the reason they listen to his intuitive political hunches is that they are—remember?—simply pieces on that infinite chessboard. Byron arranged for them to respond to him a hundred moves ago.

When he's depressed and laments not having a business card, a secretary, and a company credit card the way wet-behind-the-ears 24-year-old law school graduates do, Byron sometimes threatens to chuck the whole thing, open up a restaurant in Sante Fe, and leave Washington to the wolves. But how can he? You don't just get up from a 20- or 30-year chess career, no matter how indefinable, for the fleeting luxuries of a "title," an "occupation," and a "product" to sell.

Between chess moves, Byron wrote this book, a distillation of his unique lifestyle and a product of his even more uniquely fertile brain. The essays, whether insightful, exciting, frustrating, joyous, cynical, or shocking, are guaranteed to make you view the world in a new way. They deal with relationships and egos, love and power, elitism and politics, but they are mostly about uncertainty and change—two commodities that will not be in short supply in the

1980s, even if everything else is. Whether you pessimistically lament that nothing can be done or optimistically cheer that everything is possible, this book may provide just the necessary understanding to get through the changes and uncertainties of the coming decade.

Peter Harnik
Washington, D.C.
February, 1982

Introduction

I think of myself as a community organizer, not as a writer, for I would much rather organize my fellow citizens than write books. I am not affecting modesty when I say this, for of these two lines of work, I contend that community organizing is the higher calling The Greeks had a saying something like this: It is good to write about a thing, and better still to make a poem about it, but best of all is to do it. Community organizers are people who go out and do things. So why write about organizing when you can do it? Maybe this is why so few organizers write and why the literature on community organizing is so slight.

I am a little surprised to find this collection of essays on my hands. These beastly, impertinent creatures have a life of their own and they fought their way out of my brain and onto these pages, causing me much distress along the way. Why have they manifested themselves? They represent, I suppose, some sort of catharsis for me. A dozen years of community organizing lie behind me, years spent in the muddy trenches of a hundred civic battles. Having seen the better side of forty, some days I feel I must withdraw from this odd, grueling profession before I am reduced to mere ranting Running low on the moral fervor and certainty that fuel most organizing efforts, I am left with this question: What did I prove if anything, in all those years as a community organizer?

For all my pride in it, the vocation of community organizing is little known and less regarded in the world at large. Most people don't know it exists mainly because we organizers do not play by the rules Conventional endeavors are judged by conventional measures: in business, profit; in politics, election; in art criticism; in science, discovery; in war, victory. But community organizers, the agents of social change, have no such handy measures. We pursue no conventional goals and so we obtain no conventional rewards. Because we pursue unconventional goals, we obtain unconventional rewards. It's not a bad bargain. For one thing, we are exposed along the way to many unusual perspectives on what makes people tick and why things happen the way they do. Eventually, this adds up to quite an education. These essays are a distillation of what I have learned as a community organizer. Maybe by them the quality of my endeavors can be judged.

Now a word or two about the substance of what follows. Two basic premises, neither of them original, weave through these essays and provide, I hope, a measure of unity to the collection. The first premise is that the prevailing culture—industrialism, the age of science, patriarchy, or whatever you care to call it— is in serious decline and, if it goes, it may take the human species with it. The second premise is that our culture is on the verge of transformation, that a new age is dawning much as the Renaissance arose to transcend the Middle Ages. Though I have only borrowed these premises from others (who, incidentally, make a better case for them than I do), I take both quite seriously. As Buckminster Fuller has observed, "What we have here on the planet Earth is a nip-and-tuck situation."

Luckily for me, there is so much evidence floating around to support my basic premises that I needn't weigh you down with documentation for them. If you wish to obtain it, I hereby refer you to the nearest good bookstore where you will find shelves groaning with (a) gloom-and-doom books about impending economic/energy/ ecological disasters; and (b) counterculture books detailing, the bright promise of the new age from androgyny to Zen. Take your pick.

In these essays I set forth my own admittedly idiosyncratic variations on the themes of cultural decay and rebirth. My real-life organizing experience, I freely confess, leaves me convinced that <u>nothing can be done</u> to solve social problems by conventional means. Virtually every conventional response will actually make things worse. This is because the basic implicit assumptions on which the present system was erected have become outmoded and discredited.

Here are three examples of basic assumptions that have now turned sour.

1. <u>Centralization leads to efficiency</u>. Just a glimpse of the

morass that federal bureaucracy has become exposes how threadbare this assumption is.

2. Technology is more reliable than human beings. In other words, computers do not err; machines do not break down; systems can be made failsafe. Ask any consumer about the validity of this assumption.

3. Consumption is the path to prosperity. Whenever the economy falters, American leaders, whether liberal or conservative, always urge citizens to rush out and spend money in the belief that gorging on material goods, whether we need them or not, will keep the economy booming. This used to "work," but the cheap energy and abundant natural resources that provided massive hidden subsidies for these binges are a thing of the past. Now the chickens have come home to roost.

The assumptions of industrialism were sound enough in an earlier time, but, like all assumptions, they were only true up to a point, one we have long since passed. We are now so far removed from their original validity that to ride these assumptions farther and harder can only bring failure and suffering. Our political/economic system tends to respond to its distress by redoubling its efforts along old lines. This just digs us deeper into the hole we are struggling to get out of.

Efforts to halt or reverse the system's decline that are rooted in the old basic assumptions are obviously bound to fail for the same reasons the system itself is failing But here is the awful irony we are facing: The only efforts that the system will permit are those firmly rooted in the old assumptions. An example: When the government, after years of prodding by citizen groups, finally began to support solar energy development, it set things up so that most of the grants, contracts, and subsidies went to big institutions and corporations. Now, it so happens, big institutions and corporations do not really believe in solar energy, nor do they understand how to develop it. By its very nature, solar energy is best applied in decentralized ways. By their very nature, centralized institutions cannot comprehend decentralization. Handing over the control of solar energy's development to big companies is like asking elitists to promote the values of populists; never the twain shall meet. But big institutions and corporations mouth the assumptions recognized and trusted by the system. They are as comfortable as an old shoe so they get the financial support.

New efforts rooted in fresh assumptions will be opposed and even repressed by the prevailing system simply because this system is programmed less to learn than to endure. Accordingly, it learns poorly but endures well. If you don't think so, just try to change the system, even the tiniest bit. Try to get a traffic light installed on a corner where one is badly needed. You'll learn a lot if you do. It will probably take a couple of tragic accidents before you even stand a chance of winning. Blood sacrifice will force enlightenment upon us when the tug of common sense is inadequate to do so. As a community organizer, I took part in wave after wave of assault upon the prevailing system I may or may not have changed the system, but I know one thing for sure: I changed.

Personal growth is the key to the new age because changing oneself <u>is</u> changing the system. And people are changing in droves! All over America, people are learning how to raise not only their own vegetables, but their consciousnesses as well. They are conserving energy, preserving neighborhoods, and devising new models for community economic activity. They are building quiet, ephemeral, but powerful citizen networks to pursue their goals of sexual and racial equality, consumer and environmental protection, and economic and technological decentralization.

More of these social-change agents exist than most people realize. According to the Stanford Research Institute, more than five million Americans are now living lives of "voluntary simplicity." These people are experimenting with alternative lifestyles in countless ways. In the nature of things, most of these experiments will fail, but some of them are bound to succeed. For example, much successful work has already been completed in developing decentralized uses of solar energy. The point is, while much of this endeavor now seems grubby and too small to be significant, practical new working models are being devised for the future. If and when the worst appears—say, global famine becomes a reality, as it may—that will be the time to pass judgment on the social technological experimentation initiated by social-change advocates. Backyard fish tanks may seem laughable to people who now do their grocery shopping at the local supermarkets, but they may feel differently when food production or transportation systems falter and the supermarkets' shelves grow bare.

I deeply appreciate the fresh leadership now being provided by the hippies and housewives, citizen activists and networkers, cultural mutants and dissidents in the professions who make up the counterculture now challenging American society. They are providing _real_ leadership unlike the timid foot-dragging most of our politicans have come to offer. Since these experimenters rarely possess conventional political power, they use their own time, energy, and lives to demonstrate alternative means of shelter, food production, energy supply, education, health care, community economic development, and so on. They make these vast contributions happily for they are buoyed by the belief that _everything is possible_ if only people adapt and evolve in harmony with emerging realities.

But what a tightrope we must walk to get to the new age! Our vaunted capacity for technological innovation, even if we revive it in subtle, life-enhancing forms, will only carry us part of the way. The real trick lies not so much in devising new, socially responsible tools as in replacing an old value system that puts greed, competition, exploitation, and intolerance on top. Certainly, to get to the new age, we must be as innocent as doves, but as cunning as serpents. We human beings are still pulling along the same old bag of desperate ego hunger we have dragged through the dust of the planet since the gift of consciousness first became ours. Now, more aware than ever of our own flawed and complex nature, more aware than ever of the dangerous consequences of our violent thrashing about upon the earth, we are called upon to behave more responsibly and sensitively than we have heretofore thought possible. The situation may be grave, but our step must be light.

For openers, we must guard against our addiction to certainty. The present , as I sense it, is so verging on transformation that to be sure of anything is to court foolishness. Certainty, until now thought of as a source of strength, now appears to be a weakness, an affliction. We might as well greet uncertainty warmly. We are going to have to live with it in any case. And we can count on uncertainty to keep us on our toes.

Nobody knows where we are going, for nobody has ever been there before. But we needn t be afraid. When the Middle Ages succumbed to the Renaissance, an ancient belief system tumbled with it. Many people felt the end of the world was near. But vital new belief systems arose to replace the old one. So it is today. Let us feel our way one step at a time, taking care to be kind to one another along the way. For this journey, we need patience. not zeal; humility, not arrogance; innocence, not cynicism; and diversity, not conformity. We must be playful, inventive, and willing sometimes to play the fool. After all, if you don't know whether to laugh or to cry, it is better by far to laugh.

Confessions of a Community Organizer

"Try to do no good," advised Lord Melbourne, "and then you won't get into any scrapes." Community organizers, I fear, are born with a deaf ear to this counsel, because they are indefatigable do-gooders and thus always in scrapes. Who are these people? What motivates them? What do they get out of it?

Nature, in its bounty, seems to have programmed a few members of the human species to kick up a fuss at the first sign of oppression or abuse of authority. Whether this is done in the service of universal justice or just for the sheer hell of it, I really can't say. But nature is prudent as well as bountiful so it programmed a vastly larger number of individuals whose job it is to keep the lid on tight.

To appreciate community organizing one must perceive the need and possibility for constructive social change. Those who think the status quo is the best of all possible worlds will view community organizing with fierce hostility. Those who admit the world is a bit messy and troubled, but who fear misguided reforms more than present afflictions, will view community organizing with considerable skepticism. Those who are angry, alienated, or apathetic will view community organizing with derision and scorn. In brief, it's a wonder that some few people actually greet community organizers with warmth and cheer. But there is always a small group of hardy souls who keep alive the vision of the ideal human community and to these people community organizing, whether on a local or an international scale, seems like a sensible and desirable thing to do.

In truth, community organizing is a vital and legitimate part of our politics, one with a long and honorable history. Small radical groups have always shouldered the burden of introducing needed changes into our society. From the Boston Tea Party on—from the abolitionists to the suffragettes, from the labor organizers to the civil rights demonstrators—organizers have kicked up many a fuss and ultimately the country as a whole has come to accept their new values.

Unlike politicians, whom they resemble in some respects, organizers do not, at least in theory, seek power or office for themselves. Organizers help people try to obtain power over their own lives and communities. Thus, one basic achievement of organizers is in broadening political representation. Groups in society that are poor, outcast, or unorganized remain a slight factor to most politicians simply because they lack power. But with careful, hard work, any powerless group in society can become organized, and therefore powerful. Then politicians will be eager to represent their interests. However, it is a rare politician who will actually organize the powerless. Why should he? His aim is to win office and his function is to resolve conflicts between powerful, competing groups in society. Usually politicians are so busy mediating pressures brought to bear by the already powerful that they are unable or unwilling to seek participation from weak and unorganized groups. This is the organizer's job.

Community organizers, bless their hearts, oblivious to the fact that it probably can't be done, try to reconcile power and virtue. Somebody, I suppose, ought to keep gnawing at this eternal contradiction and I am glad that community organizers are among those who do. Other people with strong drives toward self-expression quickly detect that power and virtue do not mix, so they decide to opt for one or the other. Smith might set out to be elected president; Jones might set out to be elected pope. Very few would take aim at both targets simultaneously! But community organizers, I confess, are tantalized by a vision of a <u>just community</u> wherein the politics are clean and the clean are political. And if, in their secret heart of hearts, community organizers are envisioning themselves in the role of ruler/priest or hero/saint, so be it. Such imagery, while glorious, is also a heavy burden to drag around. Ordinary people know this and, in their simple wisdom, they exercise the best judgment of all by renouncing the pursuit of either power or virtue. A plague on both their houses! Ordinary people, very sensibly, live out their lives as decently as possible under the circumstances, burdened by neither glory nor saintliness.

Because organizers are fundamentally ambivalent about it,

"real" power usually evades their grasp. Almost by definition, a <u>good</u> community organizer couldn't be elected dogcatcher in any town in America. Organizers are simply too far ahead of the conventional wisdom to acquire the bland respectability most office-seekers embody or profess to embody. In the court of public opinion, most politicians will say only what they think the people want to hear. (I don't blame them for this; they have to be elected whereas community organizers are self-appointed.) At this court, the jesters are the community organizers who are permitted to say anything that comes into their fool heads ("nuclear power is unsafe") so long as they are willing to be the butt of jokes and to take a few hard licks now and then. On the surface, these jesters are denied "real" power, but once in a while they are able to slip a little truth (usually described as "bad news") into the public's ear. If the public gets the message and begins to shift its opinion, the politicians/courtiers scurry about revising their rhetoric and, little by little, the bad news becomes the new conventional wisdom. All in all, this arrangement works pretty well. The organizers have fun, the politicians get the credit, and social change is secured.

But community organizing is not all fun, not by any means. Sometimes the worst pain is inflicted upon organizers by their own dear brothers and sisters in the cause. You have to be highly motivated to be an organizer and motivation on this scale takes an ego of considerable proportions. No matter how diligently and sincerely they attempt to disguise it behind fine talk about "democratic control," most organizers (me included) are walking displays of egotism. In moments of despair, I have dolefully inquired of myself: Is democratic social collaboration really possible? Sometimes it is so tortuous that it doesn't seem worth the effort. Trying to define the common good can be like sticking pins into one's own flesh. I am reminded of Henry Adam's definition of democracy as "the systematic organization of hatreds."

After witnessing some especially astounding egotistical rambunctiousness on the part of my blood-sworn colleagues (my own conduct and motivation having been, I can assure you a model of blameless integrity), I have cried into my beer and lamented the fact that people are no damn good! But egotism, I have had to learn, is not just the other guy's problem, it is mine too. Ego is a blessing; it comes with the territory called life. Ego is consciousness! However, the flip side of this blessing is the curse of intolerance. We are all among the accused and the human condition makes our voyage in search of the ideal community a storm-tossed journey at best.

Here is the organizer's true lament: Everybody talks about the need for organizing, but hardly anybody does anything about it. The stance of social institutions seems to be: millions for research and education, but not one cent for organizing. Even fervent advocates of social change lend surprisingly little support to grassroots organizing. For example, left-wing intellectuals on the whole would rather do anything—debate, analyze, research, confer, write, tear each other to shreds—than organize a community. Why is this so? Maybe organizing is so mundane an activity that persons with exalted intellects fear it will dirty their hands. When I contemplate my own career, I sometimes torture myself with this question: What is the most obvious thing in the world to do if one wishes to do good? The answer: Help the neediest of the needy, as Mother Teresa does in India. Here is one little woman who is daily rendering direct assistance to starving children and dying beggars, clearly the neediest people on earth. To anyone with a social conscience as big as a thimble, the stark, clear _obviousness_ of this priority has to be overwhelming! Yet what she does is so singular, so _very_ singular, that she gets the Nobel Peace Prize for doing it. (Naturally, she contributes the prize money to the service of the poor.) I am not doing what Mother Teresa does. I don't even spend ten percent of my time in direct service to the neediest. No, but here I am writing a book. I guess I don't want to get my hands dirty, either.

On the other hand, how many people do you know who have contributed half their time over a dozen years to the service of good causes? I have done that and so have a lot of other organizers. And I am proud of it. (Oops! Watch that ego!) The question here becomes, why? What drives the organizers? Way down deep, I confess, the answer may be pure and simple resentment of authority. So what if the psychological motivation is pathetically plain to any greenhorn Freudian? So what if organizers are all trying to get even with their fathers? If nobody ever came along and stirred things up, everyone would live as serfs or slaves under the thumb of some despot. However it comes, the impulse towards social change is fundamentally desirable, even if it is sometimes mismanaged or misdirected. Human beings have been unable to resist the siren call of social change ever since we first crawled out of the primordial ooze.

Tackling the power of authority takes all the fierce egotism that organizers can muster. This David and Goliath aspect of the contest has its compensations, after all. Playing the game of life with a weak hand makes the sensation of winning ever so delicious. "To be in the weakest camp," as G. K. Chestertown observed, "is to be in the strongest school."

So Many People, So Few Populists

The visits of angels, it is said, are few and far between. So it is with our better natures. We keep them under wraps until some disaster comes along and gives us a chance to rise to the occasion. Floods, earthquakes, and other acts of God bring out the best in people and set them to cooperating with a zeal never displayed in normal times. Purely mechanical failures sometimes have the same effect. Strangers trapped in an elevator together will form instant bonds without regard to race, creed, color, or social position.

War, of course, provides the best excuse of all. In wartime, all sorts of people do noble, selfless things they would never think of doing in peacetime. When the war is over, however, people quickly revert to standard dog-eat-dog behavior and let the devil take the hindmost.

As a novice community organizer, I stumbled over this ugly truth in shock and horror. There I was going around pleading with people to sacrifice themselves for the greater good and being surprised when they turned me down. I figured something must be wrong. Heaven knows my arguments were sound. I argued about how much better things would be if only we worked together instead of against each other. I argued that there would be plenty for all, if only we shared more fairly. My case was made with a nice bit of passion and, if I do say so myself, a degree of eloquence appropriate to such sentiments. But all my pretty words fell on deaf ears. Finally, it dawned on me that there must be a catch somewhere. With so many people, I lamented, why are there so few populists?

Under the skin, most liberals and conservatives are blood-brothers. "The trouble with conservatives is that they always assume people are lazy," says anarchist Karl Hess. "And the trouble with liberals is that they always assume people are dumb." Neither group places much trust in the people themselves.

Anarchism, the idea of a society free of direct, coercive government, strongly appeals to me. Under anarchy social order would be determined through voluntary action, which is to me the highest form of social collaboration. But, much as I love it, I don't think voluntary action is equal to the full demands of human community Here is the catch: People cannot stand too much freedom, just as they cannot stand too little. If everybody were self-motivating and self-reliant, then maybe anarchy would stand a chance. But not everybody is.

When given an opportunity to realize themselves, most people either shrink from it or botch the job. We fear our hidden potential as much as we love it. In Ernest Becker's book, The Denial of Death, psychologist Abraham Maslow said that "We fear our highest possibilities. We are generally afraid to become that which we can glimpse in our perfect moments. We enjoy and even thrill to the godlike possibilities we see in ourselves in such peak moments. And yet we simultaneously shiver with weakness, awe, and fear before these very same possibilities."

In order to get from day to day, people need a firm sense of boundaries. Culture provides these boundaries. Our every thought is as dependent on this web of culture as our every breath is dependent on the web of nature. Cultural boundaries operate with great force and no one of woman born can escape them. We may sometimes resent and resist these boundaries, but we cannot shake them any more than we can shake our genetic endowment. If the system that results sometimes seems pitiless, we must remember that it is rooted in skepticism about human nature, a skepticism we all share. Alone in the jungle or forest, we may fear lions and tigers and bears. But lions and tigers and bears are not invading human communities nor are they out mugging people and driving up the crime rate. What we really fear is each other. Our culture is rooted in this fear because this fear is real.

Ordinary people understand perfectly well how the cultural system operates, but many intellectuals never perceive that they do. It is a lesson that intellectuals decline to learn But ordinary people, drawing on many worthy sources—folk wisdom, common sense and intuition, myth and tradition—observe with clear, unblinking eyes what is going on about them. In the privacy of their own minds, they make things whole and clear. They are , after all, as interested in surviving as your average Harvard Ph.D.

Few paradoxes or ironies of life escape the notice of ordinary people. They know that what we are taught to say is frequently different from what we are taught to do. They know that each of us is occasionally dragged forward and forced by the system to swallow a dose of humiliation. They know that when this happens, it does no good to complain. We are even compelled to pretend that we like it. Stiff upper lip, stout fellow!

I am convinced that, way down deep, everybody alive is nursing a little fund of secret radicalism. But I am equally convinced that no social explosions are likely to result. Ordinary people are afraid of social explosions, and in this I am in sympathy with them.

One of the first lessons I learned as a community organizer is that most people are afraid to openly express their critical, dissenting opinions. They are content to grumble and submit. In time I came to appreciate their reluctance and to see the wisdom of it. Ordinary people are not cowards nor are they fools. They keep quiet because it is the smartest thing to do. They know full well that authority is a menace always about to strike. Moreover, they know that schemes for their liberation are almost certain to fail, or at best will merely exchange new masters for old.

Consider their dilemma. With one hand, ordinary people have to resist oppressive authority while, with the other, they have to fight off schemes for their improvement and uplift by well-meaning reformers. To aid in their protection, they have learned to evade calls to action issued by zealous do-gooders. Intellectural reformers are always certain they know what to do about social problems, but ordinary people do not share this certainty. To them, reality is so complex a puzzle that no one can be sure what the outcome of a different course of action might be. Another reason that ordinary people view novel schemes with alarm is that these schemes often backfire. When they do, ordinary people are usually the ones who get burned, while the schemes' authors slink back unscorched to tenured jobs in academe or bureaucractic sinecures. It must be said that the track record of ordinary people in resisting passionate calls to action looks pretty good alongside the trash-heap of novel schemes from yesteryear.

Ordinary people know it is dangerous to go first. Suppose you have been denied a job because you are black or old or female. This injustice may be spitting in your face, but that doesn't mean anyone will join you if you fight back. You may be hurt worse if you fight back. Without allies, you are probably doomed anyway. If no one else is combatting the injustice, why should you? Let somebody else do it.

Besides, you don't really want to call the big system into question. Bad as it is, the system still delivers bread to the table. The bread may be mass-produced a thousand miles away and flown to your table at great and growing expense. It may be tasteless spongy stuff devoid of nutrients and loaded with chemical preservatives, but still it is bread. We all have to eat. People fomenting change may be full of sweet talk about how abundant and fine bread will be under a new system, but talk is cheap. Criticizing the prevailing system just might lessen its ability to keep delivering bread, however poor, to your table. Then where would you be?

If everyone began to air his or her complaints, the entire system might begin to topple. If you let too many cats out of the bag at once, where will it end? There may be no stopping until we exhaust some dark atavistic impulse and the streets are flowing with blood. No day, for example, ever dawned more brightly than that which greeted the French Revolution. After centuries of repression, freedom of speech was granted to everyone. People were encouraged to state their grievances openly in an atmosphere of "liberty, equality, and fraternity." When the curtain finally rang down on the Reign of Terror, most of the golden tongues that had launched the revolution had been silenced for all time. Ordinary people have no love of terror. They would prefer to pick their way through the mine fields of existence without encountering such dangerous excitements.

The fear that things will go too far if we take off the lid is matched by a concern about the exact opposite. This concern is that, no matter what you do, it will have no effect. You can't fight city hall. Why waste your time? Ordinary people live on more intimate terms with futility than do intellectual reformers. Intellectuals play a game that occasionally provides at least the illusion of accomplishment or even of victory. If nothing else, they can always score points off each other and call their game the search for truth. This puts the sense of satisfaction felt by intellectuals at some distance from the sense of futility experienced by ordinary people. But among the many paths to wisdom, a knowledge of futility is certainly one. I remember seeing Bertrand Russell on television shortly before his death. He was seated in an overstuffed chair and, when he wished to emphasize a point, he would make a fist and pound its arms. "You have to learn that the world is a terrible, terrible place," he exclaimed, pounding away. "Then and only then can you go out and start to become happy." Until we have learned what we cannot do, which is much, we never know what we can do. Futility represents a path to wisdom that ordinary people have traversed much farther, I suspect, than have their supposed betters. Here is one place they are scoring points off the intellectuals.

Perhaps the greatest strategic advantage ordinary people possess over their would-be benefactors is that they are not burning with the need to act. Being ordinary, they don't expect to go down in history. They are not itching for dramatic opportunities to display their genius and virtue. When a problem comes along, they are willing to ignore it in the hope that maybe it will go away. And sure enough, sometimes it does. In fact, this happens with sufficient frequency that the do-nothing option merits a greater place among our options than is usually allowed it. This sensible choice is likely to be exercised much more readily by ordinary people than by intellectual reformers. Ordinary people do not greet every crisis that comes along as an opportunity for self-glorification. They shrink from exhibiting themselves, considering such exposure indecent. But since when do ordinary people know anything about good taste?

Ordinary people are innately conservative. Properly understood, this conservatism is a way of protecting ourselves from ourselves. This protective mechanism should be appreciated for what it is by advocates of social change. If they despise and deride it, they may wind up feeling like a community organizer I once knew who complained to me that "the people" had let him down. I told him I was unaware that "the people" had ever promised to hold him up.

Of all the ideas brewing in the caldron of social ferment, only a few are actually good enough to work in complex reality. The long, arduous testing they must endure by a skeptical citizenry is natural and desirable. So if you happen to be promoting some novel scheme, don't be surprised if people don't buy it right off. And don't categorize them as a bunch of idiots for failing to appreciate your genius and virtue. Maybe you should pay more attention to the wisdom of the ordinary. "The course of every intellectual if he pursues his journey long and unflinchingly enough," said Aldous Huxley, "ends in the obvious, from which the non-intellectuals have never stirred."

How Did Outside Agitators Get Aboard the Space Colony?

A few years ago I was invited to participate in a panel discussion on the topic, "Is One World Enough?" The discussion was to be part of a conference organized by a futurist group in Washington, D. C., called the New Worlds Network. (The group's name, I thought, revealed rather guilelessly just where they stood on the question posed to the panel.) The discussion was held on a Saturday morning in October and, as it happened, the day was spectacularly bright and beautiful. As I hailed a cab to go there, I remember thinking what a shame it was to be cooped up on such a day.

At the big hotel where the New Worlds Network was located, I had some difficulty finding their offices—actually a television studio as it turned out—because they were located in a subterranean area reached by a special elevator. Finally, I found it and entered a large, dark cavern-like room punctuated by a few glaring white television lights. The program was to be videotaped. Recorded music—eerie, nerve-jangling stuff—filled the room while the audience, mostly young, hip space buffs, scraped about noisily in rows of gray metal folding chairs.

I greeted my fellow panelists and was surprised to find that there were nine or ten of us, quite a large group I thought for a panel discussion, but there we were scheduled to run from nine o'clock until noon. There would be plenty of time and, heaven knows, the topic before us merited any amount of discussion. Except for me, the panelists were well-known futurists, social critics, and academics. I felt pleased to be in such company. Maybe some distinction would rub off, making the sacrifice of the exquisite morning worthwhile.

The moderator of the discussion (and only woman participant) was Barbara Marx Hubbard, a leader of the futurist movement and an old friend of mine. It was she who had insisted that a community organizer be included in the discussion and who had invited me to come. Barbara kicked off the discussion with an eloquent advocacy of space colonization, which represents for her the logical next step in human evolution. Barbara believes that the physical resources of the solar system can and should be tapped for new scientific and economic development. Her view is that space colonies will enable us to transcend earthly limits to growth and to make a great evolutionary step forward. She then introduced the panel and laid down simple rules for the discussion: Each panelist was to have ten minutes to speak and, at the end of these presentations, the audience would be permitted to ask questions.

I happened to be the first panelist introduced and suspecting (rightly, as it turned out) that everyone else on the panel supported space colonization, I felt duty-bound to make the case against it. I said that so long as people are starving on earth, I do not see how we can justify spending billions of dollars on space technology, especially since our already vast investment has yielded so few practical social benefits. Tang breakfast drink, I observed, is not a sufficient return on our investment. I said that earth, our home, is an unusually pretty and hospitable place to live and that if we care for it as we ought to, it will remain so indefinitely. For me, I stated, the overriding issue is to preserve human life on earth in a setting of peace and justice. Once that is achieved, so far as I am concerned, they can go out and play in the cosmos to their hearts' content. Safely within my ten-minute limit, I shut up and sat down.

In the presentations that followed, there was much said that was stimulating; some of it was even brilliant. But the other speakers seemed to be primarily concerned with the <u>how</u> of space colonization rather than the <u>why</u>. Since space colonies are nearing technical feasibility, the other panelists assumed that space colonies will be built. Moreover, they assumed that these colonies will provide answers to humanity's worst problems. Overpopulation, energy and food shortages, and urban and ecological crises will wither away and so will most other ills attending our confined status on this little planet. Physically, intellectually, spiritually, we are poised on the edge of the "high frontier," the greatest challenge ever! Meanwhile, back at home base, Earth will be restored and preserved as a sort of cosmic park where weary space travelers can grab a bit of rest and recreation.

Amid such claims as these, the objections I had raised seemed paltry and irrelevant, and they sank unnoticed to the floor as wave after wave of technological optimism filled the room. Unfortunately, by the time all the speakers finished, it was half-past noon and time to adjourn for lunch. End of meeting.

Why have I recounted this story? Because the experience is typical. While it appears trivial, it reveals so much about the contradictions in human nature that I can't help wallowing in the memory of it. Contradictions in human nature are so bawdy and cheeky that there is no way for a polite observer to ignore them. If you try, they will grab you by the lapels and shout in your face. They turn up everywhere, crashing elegant parties and solemn occasions with equal bad grace. They have the worst manners imaginable, and they stalk us through every step of life.

I m sure we would agree, for example that people ought to be judged by how consistently their behavior reflects the values they espouse. That goes without saying, right? But does the zealous proponent of collective action become so angry when the collective goes against him that he tries to destroy it? Is the author of brilliant treatises advocating anarchy in fact a bully who tries to domininate every conversation? Is the passionate defender of group process actually a judgmental, intolerant person who gets a kick out of hurting other people's feelings? Is the public interest advocate who is demanding greater accountability from public agencies himself unwilling to account for what he does?

People don't like to have these contradictions called to their attention. It's as if a conspiracy exists among us all; if you don't point out my obvious inconsistencies, then I won't point out yours. Thus we all avoid being called to task for our human inadequacies, and we can all breathe a sigh of relief. But sometimes a meddlesome do-gooder comes along and breaks this conspiracy of silence by saying those things that everyone has agreed are better left unsaid, just as I did at the futurists' meeting. Everybody there declared that space colonization would inevitably lead to a better life for all people, and for this reason, they were advocating it. I know they were sincere, but how well did their behavior comport with their picture of justice for all?

Proponents of space colonization have an unbounded faith in the human ability to control technology, but they fail to note the evidence to the contrary right beneath their noses. What compelled them to turn their backs on that lovely autumn morning and gather in the bowels of a big building? The demands of technology, that's what. The video god beckoned and they submitted without delay. Otherwise, they could have met in a room with windows or even outside beneath a tree. But, not for the first time, human beings were bent to the demands of technology instead of the other way around. Wait a minute, I thought this stuff was supposed to serve us? (Stop the space colony, I want to get off!)

We don't seem to learn a lot that addresses basic human flaws. New technologies are always unveiled as liberators of humanity and we always accept this assertion at face value. When the adverse consequences of the latest dream machine start to pile up, we are genuinely surprised and let down. I know they have brought good too, but look at all the bad impacts of automobiles, television, computers, and nuclear power. Now we are told by those favoring space colonization that space technology will liberate us, this time for sure!

Chasing seductive images of the future may offer some satisfactions, but the alleviation of human want is not likely to be one of them. The chase does offer new adventure and challenge to human ingenuity and I don't wish to deny this avenue of growth and self-expression to anyone. It also offers an opportunity to have a lot of fun and I don't mean to be a spoilsport. I might even be convinced that the fun involved is the best reason for the chase. But I have to ask at what price these opportunities come? Shall we feed the many who are hungry, or shall we allow a few some supreme adventure?

The answer to this question is not as easy or as obvious as I once thought. Our evolutionary destiny may lie in space and humans (some of them, anyway) will insist that the species extend itself as far as technology will carry it. Being human, they will pursue these dreams with courage and imagination. But if service to humanity is the aim, I can point to countless opportunities for good work right here on earth. While society is being urged, in the name of human betterment, to spend trillions on space colonies, the needy all around us are becoming worse off.

I wish space buffs would search their motivation on this score and admit that technology is not the grand benefactor of the poor and needy they claim to be. People promoting hardware for space exploration have some good arguments and they should sell their product on these merits: romance, adventure, intellectual challenge, technical virtuosity. Maybe then people like me wouldn't automatically oppose their schemes. But so long as they invoke the poor on earth as the justification for their derring-do, then I'll fight them every step of the way.

While over-estimating technology's benefits, space buffs compound their error by discounting human flaws. The human species is flawed; otherwise, we would have instituted heaven on earth long ago and, clearly, we are still far from it. These human failings are so obvious that not even a child is caught by surprise by them. But, despite their obviousness, these failings play small part in the calculations of the technological optimists. They are labeled "politics" and put out of sight. Nothing must detract from the glittering images the technologists are promoting. So they offer us such things as infinite, cheap energy in the guise of nuclear power. But we have learned that the more complicated a technology, the more vulnerable it is, not only technically, but socially.

There are only two ways to guard against this vulnerability. One is to devise additional technologies as fallback systems if the primary system fails to operate. The catch is this: The fallback system adds more complexity. There are now more things that can go wrong. We all know Murphy's Law: If something can go wrong, it will. (The technological optimists overlook this universal truth, too.) Fallback systems, soothing as they appear, increase the vulnerability of technology.

I remember hearing a radio interview with a retired Federal Aviation Administration safety inspector following a terrible airplane crash. He was asked how such things could happen in this age of advanced technology. The inspector, who had been studying airplane accidents since the thirties, said that the chief reason is that every time a defect is identified as the cause of an accident, a technological system is designed and installed to eliminate that defect. Eventually this new system itself fails, causing an accident, and then some remedy for it has to be devised. Ultimately, so many systems with so many potential malfunctions evolve, that the control of human beings flying the craft is significantly diminished. When technical complexity exceeds human understanding, we have little choice but to place faith in this strange new god of our own devising.

The second defense against the vulnerability of complex technologies is to erect elaborate security systems. If these are technological (cameras, alarm systems) they are vulnerable in the same way fallback systems are. If these systems employ humans as guards, they run the risk of human failings, ranging from laxity or incompetence to treason or madness. Moreover, those paid to provide security are frequently the ones who breach it. Inside jobs are the order of the day; the security guards are the thieves. In some American cities, for example, firemen are paid more when they are fighting fires than when they are not. I am told that, if business is slow, certain firemen exercise a bit of old-fashioned ingenuity and go out and start fires. The point is that "security" cannot really be purchased. If you have a vulnerable, complex technology in your possession, it is a bit like owning the Hope diamond. A curse is upon you.

Look again at the space colonies. Who will build, operate and occupy them? Human beings, and in any group of human beings there will be a few programmed by nature to play with matches. The outside agitators aboard the space colony will be us, you or me or one of the kids, or maybe Uncle Fred who's been acting funny lately. People need not be terrorists or maniacs to threaten or disturb the delicate functions of space technology. Perfectly ordinary people have fierce disagreements all the time, sometimes with disastrous results. Take something as basic as marriage. Nobody goes into a marriage without sincerely believing it will work. Swept along by love and romance, powerfully reinforced by culture, religion, and law, two people swear to "love and honor till death do us part." But even with all this going for it, the institution of marriage is in grave disarray. Over half of all marriages in the United States now end in divorce. And other social relationships not cemented as well as marriage—business associations, political alliances, friendships--fall apart even more quickly and easily.

An organizer soon learns two things about people. One, they cannot get along without each other; two, they cannot get along with each other. Is it any wonder then that social collaboration is so hard to achieve? When even the Eden of God's own devising succumbed to human failings, how can mere mortals devise artificial environments immune to them?

Space colonization buffs forget that simple rules are hard to obey and complex rules almost impossible. One of the reasons that futurism is such an enjoyable game is that the players assume that, in the future, we will all be virtuous. God knows we all intend to be but there are a few obstacles in our way, to name seven: pride, lust, envy, anger, covetousness, gluttony, and sloth.

While we wait for this glorious, imminent transformation when we all become virtuous, we are compelled to collaborate with each other using the humble means now at our disposal. All we have to do is to muddle through without blowing up the planet. At a minimum, this requires us to establish a few rules to ensure a modicum of social justice so that most people, despite some reluctance, will support the social system. But even minor forms of social collaboration are hard to secure.

Take the apparently trivial matter of the time limit on presentations at the "Is One World Enough?" panel discussion. It was the simplest of rules, crystal clear and eminently fair, was it not? So why did all but two of the speakers break the rule by running overtime? A couple of panelists talked more than thirty minutes each. Only the moderator (a woman) and I (a community organizer) stayed within the agreed-up time limit. The other speakers, honorable gentlemen all, still managed, each and every one of them, to violate the ground rules. How does this happen? I suspect that when each of them was speaking, something like this ran through his mind: "What I am saying is so fresh and important that no one will mind if I go over the time limit just a little bit; besides, I can sense that the audience wants to hear more from me and I have only just begun to make my point."

How important are these infringements of etiquette? To me, they reveal in miniature the ageless, intrinsic conflict between individual self-expression and the ideal of community. If mature, intelligent, well-meaning, and responsible people in a civilized setting of free inquiry cannot obey a simple rule, how can we expect them to obey complex rules in an artificial, highly vulnerable setting?

Maybe the only people allowed aboard the space colony will be supremely well-adjusted white males—brave, courteous, fit, trained, a publicist's dream—like the astronauts were supposed to be. But how does such a screening fit with the ideal of community and the fact of our diversity? Besides, I'm not so sure I'd bet any more on the astronaut types than I would on any other, no matter how boyishly handsome and blandly ingratiating they happen to be. As their story trickles out, it seems that the astronauts were as infected as the rest of us with human failings.

Come to think of it, allowing any human beings aboard the

space colony is asking for trouble. Even if we establish degrees of regimentation undreamed of by the Hitlers and Stalins of the world, we cannot achieve the ideal community through hardware no matter how much of it there is. Then why do we allow the technological optimists to peddle and promote space colonies as if they were "floating Marin Counties in the sky," to borrow the apt phrase coined by Hazel Henderson, author of The Politics of the Solar Age.

Finally, it is worth noting that the self-absorption of my fellow panelists in their own preachments eliminated any chance the audience had to ask questions or to make comments. It happens more often than not that the eminent are permitted to run off at the mouth at the expense of the public's right to participate. But nobody in the audience complained. I sensed, maybe accurately, that this particular audience was too hooked on technological imagery to care. Except for me, the panelists gave them plenty of imagery to consume. A veritable feast was laid out for them while, by comparison, all I offered was cold gruel. Perhaps I should be grateful I was not booed off the stage.

Afterward I realized how much power these futuristic visions hold for people. Rather than confront the paradoxes contained in human nature, we opt for some alluring scheme that diverts us from the dreary aspects of the human condition. Maybe we should be grateful for these technological diversions. They offer a little relief from our anxiety and allow us to dream. And surely it is better to joyride through space than to engage in nuclear war. If the high-technology crowd must have a game to play—and I suppose they must—it's better they are kept busy on space hardware than on new weapons systems. If the choice boils down to that, then I'm ready, boys! Reserve me a berth on the starship. Just give me a chance to buy a jar of Tang and grab my copy of Robert's Rules of Order, and off we'll go.

Two Cheers for the Founding Persons

Is society's present anxiety simply par for the course of human events, or is it something exceptional? I suppose the inhabitants of every age assume that their brief span of consciousness happens to coincide with the principal watershed of history, but even allowing for this egocentric blindspot, the present time certainly <u>seems</u> like a turning point.

Within the last century, society has experienced the vigorous youth of industrialism, a confident, expansive order with the sky for a limit, or so it seemed. Then we experienced industrialism's portly middle age. Now we seem to be witnessing industrialism's dotage. Is the prevailing social order sinking into decline? If so, does this also mean the decline of civilized life, political freedom, and material well-being?

As historical eras go, the industrial age is rather short-lived. It is only a couple of hundred years old, just a blink of the eye on the face of time. However historically brief, industrialism has been around long enough to erase from most people's minds any recollection of other eras just as well suited to human purpose and convenience. Americans in particular have been persuaded that, thanks to science, we inhabit a golden age, the very pinnacle of human experience (a dangerous place to be, if you ask me; you cannot sit on a pinnacle forever -- it gets uncomfortable -- and you have no place to go but down!). Up to now, we have been taught, the human past was unrelieved discomfort and deprivation, with no air conditioning in the summer and no electric heat in the winter. Imagine, we are told, people in medieval towns threw their slops right out the window, sometimes drenching hapless passersby. Ugh, how disgusting! But today's cities are swimming in the filth of industrial pollution that settles in our lungs and vital organs and <u>stays there</u>. I don't know about you, but given a choice, I'd rather be drenched by somebody's chamberpot than get cancer.

Besides, every medieval city worthy of the name had a cathedral or was building one, designed to last the centuries. These still inspire awe, even to our modern God-denying eyes. In my opinion, nothing we are building today deserves to last a fortnight. And even large medieval cities, crowded though they may have been, had nature close by. For example, until the Industrial Revolution, any poor urchin in London could stroll to nearby fields, streams, and forests seeking recreation and natural beauty. Today, even rich city kids can't do that.

We need to be reminded that civilized life, political freedom, and material well-being existed before industrialism. Of course, not everyone living in the past was blessed with abundance, but then the manifold assurances of industrialism on this score haven't been fulfilled either. Industrialism's achievement has been not so much in creating material well-being as in altering our conception of what it comprises. In our time, prosperity may be defined as the number of carcinogenic products one owns. The more electric hair dryers, microwave ovens, color televisions, and automobiles, the better. Somehow I can't get too excited about this golden age.

Yes, I know that great advances have been made in such fields as medicine and I gratefully acknowledge them. If I get a brain tumor and modern medicine removes it, leaving mind and body restored, I 'll be grateful to be living in the age of science. And I do know that physicians in the past employed unbelievably crude, barbarous techniques that often did more harm than good. But modern physicians do the same thing in their own way. Each year, thousands and thousands of operations are performed not because they are necessary to health, but because they provide highly remunerative employment for surgeons. This smacks of barbarity to me.

The truth is that life is not a long natural upward progression culminating conveniently in our time. This view is a fundamental misreading of history and it astonishes me how widespread it is. Most people really do think we are living at the pinnacle! And most people also think we are about to fall off, which is why they are so depressed and anxious. But neither impression is correct. The past is not to be despised; it wasn't so bad. And the future is not to be feared. We may have to live without aluminum foil and such, but we can manage.

Creation is not so unjust as to consign all previous generations to the status of mere stage-setters for our star turn in the human comedy. Maybe they didn't have penicillin, but they had means for enjoying life. According to historian Paul Murray Kendall, ordinary people in fifteenth-century England spent less time laboring than people do now. Because religion was foremost in society, they celebrated it constantly. Practically every week brought one saint's day or another to be celebrated with parades, festivals, and solemn rites; the very word holiday comes from holy day. Life in the fifteenth century couldn't have been so bad, even if people were tossing slops on each other.

To my reading, human history seems more like a series of ebbs and flows than a long progression upward. You win a few and you lose a few; we advance in one dimension and retreat in another. People used to build cathedrals, now they build glass boxes. People used to die before they reached forty, now life begins there. There is a rhythm to this change and we would be wise to dance to the beat that time has chosen. Always, the trick is to strike a new balance amid changing conditions.

This is where the Founding Persons—that wonderful band of American revolutionists—come in. They had their fingers on the pulse of history and they picked up the right beat. In part, they were able to do this because their life experiences had been particularly instructive. Perhaps no other generation of people who ever lived were as free as the American revolutionaries. Their forebears and they hacked a new life out of the wilderness and, if they still depended on the Old World for luxuries, they achieved a hard-won self-reliance. They learned to innovate; Yankee ingenuity and American know-how were to become bywords all over the globe. It is worth noting, by the way, that the Americans' material independence preceded their political independence, though it was equally hard-won. When it came time to write a constitution, they drew upon their unusual experience and produced a conception of government that is still impressive.

The Constitution was a valiant attempt to strike a new balance within dynamic circumstances. I admire the result because it dealt wisely with the contradictions in human nature. Conflicting impulses motivate us all, complicating and impeding our social and political relations, and sometimes resulting in bloody strife and turmoil. The framers of the Constitution were intimately familiar with these human flaws and they astutely sought to bring them into balance.

The fundamental impetus for democracy derives from an impulse that animates the human species: the impulse toward creativity, toward freedom, self-expression, spontaneity, diversity, innovation, and change. These are lovely qualities and life would be unthinkable without them. But there is another animating impulse, one tending toward stability, toward wisdom. It, too, is associated with many laudable qualities: order, tradition, excellence, competence, craft, restraint, discipline. What would life be without these?

Both impulses motivate us as individuals and as groups, but they function in contrasting ways. Sometimes they appear to be competing or in conflict. For example, we might enjoy being surprised once in a while, but we would dislike being surprised constantly. Balance is necessary.

The impulse toward freedom generates growth and change, thus it always calls authority into question and challenges old practices. But carried to excess, this impulse leads to confusion, disorder, and sometimes to violence. Nobody wants mob rule. It is worth noting that Robespierre the Incorruptible who presided over the Reign of Terror was one of the sincerest democrats who ever lived.

The impulse toward freedom recognizes that people are capable of behaving like angels, while the impulse toward wisdom recognizes that people more often behave like devils. Too much order, however, is repression. Too much stability is stagnation.

The point is that people desire both freedom and wisdom.

People wish to know where their next meal is coming from, but they also hope for a better life, which means change. The eternal dilemma is how to pursue both change and stability.

The balance struck by the framers of the Constitution was admittedly imperfect. The biggest blot on the achievement was the condoning of slavery. And since they were nearly all wealthy men with a vested interest in property rights, they restricted suffrage to land-owning white males. By contemporary standards, they failed in these respects and in some others, but I cannot join radical historians in denouncing the Founding Persons as merely a bunch of early capitalist pigs. Maybe they were conservative and propertied, but they also risked their necks and fortunes by making a revolution together, and this is a highly instructive experience not always available to ruling elites.

Their pioneer learning and revolutionary experience taught the Founding Persons much about human failings and the limitations of institutions. They were shrewd enough to know that a system that unfairly favors stability over change will itself become unstable in time. The extraordinary amount of change that the American Constitution has absorbed since its creation is a tribute to the sagacity of its authors. But smart as they were, the Founding Persons could see only dimly into the future.

At the same time America was rising to nationhood, another fledgling historical force was gathering steam, both literally and figuratively: the Industrial Revolution. The American Revolution and the Industrial Revolution were about two different things. Primarily, the colonists fought to win the right of self-government. Industrialism, at least as the early economists saw it, was pursued in the hope that it would bring society greater material security. (It didn't hurt any when some people figured out that industrialism was a good way to make money.) Fate decreed that the consequences of these two revolutions would intermingle over time to create a special brand of history in America.

The Founding Persons knew much about human nature, politics, philosophy, agriculture, commerce, and even about science. But they did not, and could not, see the coming of giant industry. They knew wealth, of course. But the wealth they knew was that of prosperous merchants, traders, and farmers. They could not envision the appearance of wealth in the fabulous concentrations that some of their grandsons would possess. Certainly, they did not foresee the emergence of huge industrial systems for providing food, water, energy, and other basic necessities of life. And they could not possibly foresee the collusion of vast wealth and high technology in a conspiracy to undermine their proudest handiwork, the Constitution of the United States.

To Repeal the Constitution, Press This Button

The greatest form of power in a democracy is and always has been wealth. This was true in the Greek city-states, in Florence during the Renaissance, and in revolutionary Philadelphia. This was also true in the small Ohio town where I grew up. Sure, people got to vote on a regular basis, but everybody understood that a small group of prosperous men—merchants, bankers, lawyers—actually ran the town. The village idiot knew this, the town drunk knew this, and all the little children in school knew this. But it was not talked about publicly.

The citizens of the town endured this oligarchy without loud complaint because they were afraid to offend the ruling clique. Soreheads would find it harder to get credit from the merchant, loans from the banker, and equal protection under the law from the police. Only in the privacy of one's family or circle of friends could one safely discuss the power structure and its defects and abuses.

Of course, we were taught to revere the Constitution and so we did. The village idiot revered it, the town drunk revered it, and all the little children in school revered it. It was the Constitution that made us free.

In America, we have a tripartite form of federal government established by our Constitution. We are told to pay careful attention to its workings and to participate, as specified, in its processes because they are the principal determinants of national life and the future. Look, we are told, the election of a president is an act of the greatest possible consequence! Keep your eyes glued on that process. But what about decisions made behind the closed doors of corporate boardrooms? They often determine the quality of life and the future more powerfully than any election does. Shouldn't we keep an eye on those processes too?

The system of power based on wealth is less respectful of the niceties than the constitutional system is, and its operations, being less open to view, are much more expedient, ruthless, and cynical. Maybe for these reasons, the constitutional system of power is frequently subordinated to the system based on wealth. Now this is an old story and it should come as no surprise to anyone age ten or over. It seems to be the timeless order of things in human communities and, within certain confines, it can be endured. Oh, if you wish you can rebel or drop out or seek to defy or evade the system in some other way, but it catches up with you sooner or later. No matter what you do, the system endures. In fact, it endures so well that, after you have fought it a while, you begin to develop a certain reluctant admiration for its crass indomitability.

Though the power system based on wealth can be and often is corrupt and venal, we must recall that its origins are not entirely disreputable. Capitalism, when operating at small or intermediate scales, has a lot of appeal for me and it seems well suited to American culture (though not to others, let me hasten to add). The nation's economic wealth and technological prowess are attributed, rightly I think, to Yankee ingenuity and American know-how. But I also think that ingenuity and know-how are inextricably linked to the small-scale enterprise that dominated our economy during much of our early history. Big businesses may be capable of exploiting innovations, but they are not capable of devising them. (Bell Laboratories may be an exception, but then the telephone company is the only monopoly for which I have any affection.)

At the entrepreneurial scale, I am prepared to live with capitalism and even with its contradictions because they happen to mirror some contradictions in human nature that I now perceive as ineradicable. I am resigned to a certain degree of greed, corruption, exploitation, and oppression just so long as it doesn't get out of hand. But how, in God's name, do you contain it?

Prosperous citizens living in a small town or city might preempt for themselves powers and prerogatives beyond the political constitution, but they are nevertheless hemmed in by some powerful constraints. For one thing, they live in the same community they control. They breathe the same air, drink the same water, and walk down the same streets as do other citizens. They are not absentee landlords remote from the consequences of their acts. At the community scale, people exercising power do so with a certain moral approbation from their fellow citizens. To be sure, such approbation is mixed with resentment and fear, but clearly there is an attitude that says: "Okay, you've grabbed power through your money. Somebody has to handle it, so we'll not complain too loudly so long as you remember to respect the outward forms of our democracy and not abuse your power. If you handle it carefully, not raking off too much for yourself, then you may hold power with our approval and even with our esteem."

Now it just so happens that the town fathers enjoy receiving the moral approbation of their fellow citizens. It makes them feel good about themselves. True, they also enjoy being feared and envied, but for the moment, we are trying to look at the bright side of this otherwise dreary picture. If the town fathers misuse or abuse their power, then things may get out of hand and they may lose face and the implied esteem of the community is withdrawn. This is painful to them and the fear of it acts as a curb on the use of their power.

The chieftains of great corporations are not as dependent on community sanctions as are local ruling elites. They are not surrounded by fellow citizens, but by fawning subordinates, mere yes-men. The decisions they make will affect many communities they never even visit, let alone inhabit. The difference is very great and, to my mind, it is largely one of scale.

Our constitutional system has been thrown out of whack not by capitalism, but by capitalism run amok. The Constitution was devised by small-scale capitalists who saw this form of economic activity as entirely consistent with their political vision. Because communication and transportation systems were few and primitive, they assumed that political and economic decentralization was the natural, inevitable state of affairs. Thus, some of the root assumptions of industrialism—consumption, conformity, centralization—are at war with the spirit of the Constitution, which is based on the assumption of a high degree of local self-reliance and regional and economic diversity.

So long as the economic system operated within the constitutional system, a rough sort of balance existed to ensure that basic freedoms were intact. Sure, local rich men had more power than other citizens, but I honestly see no answer to that.

Today, the real trouble is that the power based on wealth has so far outscaled the power of the constitutional system. The industrial system is so big and barreling down the highway so fast that all politics can do is chase after it, demanding that it curb its worst abuses. Government has grown because most citizens insist that it manage and reduce the vast social consequences of rampant industrialism. But this is a race our constitutional system is hard pressed to win. The real need is to reduce the size and complexity of the industrial system. We need to devolve it to a simpler, more comprehensible form so that the constitutional system can catch its breath and begin to work again. Doing this is a tall order, I know, and I don't have any easy answers as to how to do it. But we might be more impelled to try if we recognized that our basic liberties may be at stake.

When I was growing up in Ohio, I remember my parents and their friends and neighbors debating local political issues. If the county proposed to improve the bridge over Turtle Creek, everybody could and did confidently form his or her own judgment on whether the improvement was needed and on the reasonableness of the estimated costs. They may have judged rightly or they may have judged wrongly; the point is, they were confident of their ability to judge. Today, the issue in the same county is nuclear power and few citizens feel confident to judge it. Their common-sense experience doesn't seem equal to the myriad complexities of the technology.

Even the town fathers, once so in control of local matters, are confused and uncertain about what to do. They are up a creek along with everybody else.

Nuclear power raises many agonizing ethical questions that place great stress on constitutional systems. For example, what do we do with the wastes from nuclear power plants? They will remain radioactive for tens of thousands of years. What a deadly curse to place on future generations! But it is very difficult to assert ethics in the debate over energy policy. There is no hard data to support ethical stands and so ethical stands are inadmissible. No wonder citizens are so mystified. They are not allowed to be ethical, which they know <u>how</u> to be, but they are allowed to be scientific, which they do <u>not</u> know how to be.

Godless science in the United States, like godless communism in the Soviet Union, has evolved into an official state religion. For example, an eminent physicist, Dr. Alvin Weinberg has proposed the creation of "technological priesthoods" to solve the problems in handling and storing nuclear wastes. Since science rose at least in part as a reaction to cant and superstition in religion, I always assumed that priestly functions were somehow anathema to the practitioners of science. For my part, I would not trust a technological priesthood any farther than I could throw one. I have enough trouble trying to keep an eye on the member of Congress I help to elect; I don't have time to keep track of some technological priest whom I would have no say in electing, but who would make decisions about things vital to my survival and well-being.

I only wish Dr. Weinberg would reveal what provisions in the Constitution permit such unaccountable concentrations of power. Such proposals are not only inherently anti-democratic, they are typical of the foolishness that surrounds the whole field of nuclear power. Not long ago a corporate think tank, in exchange for a sizable chunk of taxpayers' money, provided the Energy Department with recommendations for forestalling sabotage at nuclear power plants. Among them was a proposal that every nuclear facility employ a full-time psychologist whose job it would be to keep an eye on other employees in order to detect any signs of disaffection. When I reported this to a fellow organizer, he revealed on the spot that he had a proposal for the Department of Energy that he would provide for one tenth of the fee paid to the think tank. His proposal was that every nuclear facility employ a full-time astrologer whose job it would be to track the movement of the planets. ("Better shut down number three, Al. Jupiter is in conjunction with Mars again.")

The use of big complex technologies within the industrial system is beginning to make the constitutional system look pretty frail. Nuclear power is the best example, but it is not the only one: automobile, television, and computer technologies are just three other examples of technologies that present many environmental and social problems the Founding Persons could never have foreseen. The attempt of government to subdue the ever-expanding force of industrialism by expanding itself has grown ludicrious. But if government is called off the task, then who is to protect us from unrestrained assaults by the system of power based on wealth? And what happens if the overreaching, overextended industrial system begins to falter and cease providing its massive flow of products and services? If all the lights go out on industrialism, the Constitution may not be worth the paper it is written on. There we will be, bereft not only of the benefits of industrialism but of our liberties as well.

Revival, Not Reform

Historian Walter Karp, author of The Politics of War, offers a highly plausible interpretation of American history that contrasts the concept of the republic with that of the nation. The revolutionaries, having won their freedom, established a republic, the central, fundamental purpose of which, according to Karp, was simply to permit free citizens to live their lives as they wished, uncoerced by state power. That was the entire point of the republic, not global power and influence, not national glory, and not service to, or worship of, the state.

This republic, the America of family farms, villages, and small towns and cities, survived largely intact until about the time of the Spanish-American War in 1898, a foreign and imperialistic venture that challenged the very roots of the republic and manifested the rising new force of American nationalism. As Karp views it, the nation subverts the many virtues of the republic—simplicity, localism, self-reliance—while pursuing the image of state power.

Citizens are no longer permitted to go about their business pretty much as they please; now they are expected to march off to foreign wars and to die gladly for an abstraction called the nation. Thus, patriotism that actually means love of one's country (in the sense of home, "of things familiar and formative " as Karp puts it) becomes subverted into the worship of something cold, remote, demanding and intimidating: the nation. The cult of the nation that emerged in the 1890s needed some sacred regalia and so it unfurled the American flag and trotted out Uncle Sam in an effort to give the cold abstraction of the nation some life. (The nation, Karp observes, has no legal existence; what exists under the Constitution is the republic.) Neither the flag nor the symbol of Uncle Sam had enjoyed any such status before.

The nation of the United States became a great world power. The early republicans would have found this rise to power terrifying since it could occur only at the expense of the liberties that the republic was constituted to preserve. "We were citizens of the republic " Karp notes, "long before we ever saw ourselves as members of a nation. In the early days of the republic, the very word nation, innocuous in itself actually offended fastidious republicans. They detected an aroma of despotism about it, and they were not, it turns out, all that far wrong."

Despite decades of world power and a military and foreign policy predicated on goals of "national" aggrandizement and dominance, the republic, Karp is relieved to point out, survives still just beneath the tense, thin surface of the nation. Indeed, it should be remembered that the struggle of the republic to oppose the onslaughts of the nation was a brave, mighty one that lasted for decades. There was massive resistance to our participation in the Spanish-American War and to the acquisition of the Philippine Islands afterward. There was also massive resistance to our entry into the First World War President Woodrow Wilson, relishing his crack at a place in history as a great world leader, had to drag us into it kicking and screaming and even at that had to employ plenty of deception. (You'll remember that he won reelection in 1916 on the motto, "He kept us out of war." Having won, he turned around and took us into it, with the vast cooperation, it must be said, of the nationalist press and the Republican Party.)

Today when such disasters as the Vietnam War or Watergate (both crises of the "imperial presidency") beset us, the stress on the nation is so great that it is forced to open up and reveal the still-existent, venerable republic. Everywhere freedom-loving citizens rise up and organize themselves to curb such abuses and excesses of state power. It's no wonder that presidents are no longer elected to a second term. The republic keeps tossing them out. Eisenhower, the last president to serve two terms, was committed to doing as little as possible in office. He was wildly popular throughout his two terms and could have easily been elected to a third term in 1960.

What fueled the rise of American nationalism in the late nineteenth century and gave it the momentum to ride roughshod over the plain, but hardy virtues of the republic? Walter Karp doesn't say so, but to me it was plainly the rampart industrialism of the time. Big business with its huge appetite for raw materials, its need for large numbers of trainable, manageable, docile workers and its ceaseless search for ever larger markets found itself at war with the independent spirit, the teeming diversity and the self-reliant simplicity of the republic. Big business, in order to make its complex, long term plans, to purchase and exploit vast amounts of natural resources, to manufacture and transport its products and then to promote and sell them, must take the form of a large, complicated organizational structure and must reorganize society in this image as well. Furthermore, the abuses of big business eventually compel society to demand that government correct them. But if the government, for example, is to secure industrial pollution control, then it too must develop a large, complicated organizational structure, just to get on top of the problem. So big business gives rise to big government.

Eventually, centralization, conformity, and consumption—the imperatives of industrialism—must, of necessity, replace the republican virtues of local self-reliance, cultural and regional diversity, and material simplicity. Indeed, these virtues must even be discredited if the people are to worship the new gods placed before them by industrialism.

I see it as no accident that the rampant industrialism of the late nineteenth century induced a rampant nationalism as well. It's no accident either that this new nationalism found its outlet in an aggressive foreign policy. What else were we to do with all this newly concentrated wealth and power if not seek glory and domination over others? This is what made America "great." Right?

Well, there's another version of how American greatness originated, one that I favor. Just as there is a strong connection between the rise of the nation and the rise of industrialism so there is a strong connection between the liberties enjoyed in the republic and the amount and quality of enterprise within society. Yankee ingenuity, American know-how: These are the qualities that led to America's economic might and technological prowess, as Professor Elting Morrison points out in his book, From Know-How to Nowhere. These qualities originated not in the nation but in the republic. They preceded the rise of the nation and they made its rise possible. It's ironic that the nation in its vastness tends to oppress the very enterprising spirit to which it owes its existence.

The republic nourished the spirit of enterprise. Because within the republic, one could better one's life through hard work, thrift, and pluck, millions of small businesses appeared throughout the land. They were devoted to every conceivable purpose, high and low, good and bad, serious and silly. (To admire the republic, you have to acquire a taste for diversity, knowing well that diversity will inevitably contain many things you dislike.)

The republic also fostered an intellectual freedom, a willingness to experiment and to run risks that laid the groundwork for American science that is still, for all its many flaws and corruptions, held in awe and respect worldwide. Americans seemed born to innovate while the rest of the world looked on in amazement.

Today, as the industrial economy lurches downward, it seems to me that what the world needs now is not more production, the goal of the anxious nation, but more innovation, a function of the republic. It's been well established that the process of innovation is closely associated with small-scale enterprise. A 1976 report of the National Science Foundation estimated that the total number of innovations produced by small firms is far greater than that produced by large firms. Small companies and independent innovators account for something like two thirds of all innovations.

Society, if it is to transcend the decline of industrialism, must have a steady stream of social and technical innovations that will enable us to meet basic human needs in new ways. The republic is the best form of political organization for ensuring that this innovation takes place. To survive with our economy and technology intact perhaps we <u>must</u> revive it.

The republic is astir in any case. A phenomenal amount of experimentation is taking place at grassroots levels. Alternative energy, shelter, agriculture, transportation, education, health care—the entire self-help movement—are themes percolating throughout American society right now as the devolution of the industrial economy compels people to reassume control over their destinies. Ask not what America can do for you; ask what you can do for yourself.

The revival of the ideal of community self-reliance and the new spirit of enterprise and innovation at the grassroots suggest to me that the good old republic has a lot of life left in it still. It's become politically attractive to sound the theme of the republic too. Ronald Reagan has done it with great success even though his programs and policies ultimately serve the interests of centrist big business. Since Reagan must betray the republic politically all the while he sings its praises rhetorically, I think social change constituencies should attempt to capture that rhetoric from him and run with it themselves.

Remember, the republic is lovable whereas the nation is not. It is possible to celebrate the republic with genuine pride and joy. It is the land we love, the traditions we cherish, the history we're proud of, and our sturdiest hope for the future.

I read somewhere once that "it is always easier to revive something than to reform something." My organizing experience has taught me that there's a lot of truth in this statement. The thing you can revive is <u>real</u>. It has a life of its own; it is already there waiting to be revived. The reform you attempt to bring about has had no prior existence. You are trying to bring something new into being and that is very difficult. So instead of seeking to reform the nation, why not attempt to revive the republic?

Don't Confuse Me with the Facts

Facts are not what they are cracked up to be. Viewed cosmically, if I may be permitted such a lofty view, facts are not hard little blocks of absolute, unchanging truth, but fleeting, even flimsy things. If, for example, you tell me "The earth is round; that is a fact," then I might ask, "Was the earth always round? Will it always be?"

Up to a point, science can measure and count physical objects as they are presently constituted. Thus we know the earth is round, not flat, that it revolves around the sun and not vice versa, and that it is a member of a family of planets, and not alone. This work of science is commendable and useful and I am glad we know such things. But knowing them is not to know everything, not by a long shot.

It is convenient to regard the present roundness of the earth as a fact, but this determination has as much to do with human convenience as it has to do with truth. For our purposes, the earth is round and always has been and always will be. Conceptualizing on a broader time frame—before there was an earth or after there is none—makes a lot of people nervous for it tends to reduce the importance of humanity in the universal order. The universe is a big place, bigger in some ways than we mortals can bear, so it is understandable that in our anxiety we wish to reduce infinity to manageable proportions.

But we don't have to agree on what is manageable and, as a matter of "fact," we don't. For those who find refuge in a passel of narrow little facts, I offer congratulations. Just don't ask me to share your hiding place. I prefer to wander farther afield, exploring consciousness without having to drag along a lot of excess baggage full of facts.

While I am willing to take my hat off to science, gratefully acknowledging its achievements, I leave my hat on in the presence of the so-called social sciences. The application of science to the governance of the species is so dismal a failure that we would be better off it it had never been attempted.

The relationship of the social sciences to real science is a parasitic one and the parasites are thriving.

The social sciences provide most of the facts upon which much public policy is based. But when it comes to public policy, I would much prefer to see evidence of wisdom rather than evidence of facts. The facts of economics, psychology and sociology somehow fail to add up to wisdom. "Science robs men of wisdom," said Miguel di Unamuno, "and usually converts them into phantom beings loaded up with facts." Today, public policy is smothered in facts but devoid of wisdom. Wisdom comes hard, facts come easy. The pursuit of the ideal—truth, beauty, justice—gives rise to wisdom. Ideal qualities such as these are not subject to quantification. They cannot be counted or measured. Alongside these qualities, the facts being manufactured in such profusion by the social sciences are rude little beasts being given far too much attention.

I am not suggesting that rational analysis has no part to play in public policy. Rather, I am saying that rational analysis has often been abused and debased to the point that it is virtually exhausted. One example of how social planning can go awry is found in public housing. Once the bright hope of a whole generation of government social planners and scientists intent on providing model environments for people, public housing has instead become almost the opposite: sterile, cold, ugly complexes that are now unsafe and unsanitary. Rational analysis as applied to public policy can take us no further, so maybe we had better stop over relying on it long enough to ask what other tools are available to us.

Descartes started all this trouble by stating, "I think, therefore I am." He might just as accurately have said, "I feel, therefore I am." Both statements are equally true. Reason and feeling combine in our beings to make us human. We walk on both legs, we work with both hands, we see through both eyes: Why can't we employ both reason and feeling simultaneously? When it comes to public policy, feelings are treated as out of place. Robertson Davies, the Canadian novelist, has remarked, "We have educated ourselves into a world from which wonder, and the fear and dread and splendor and freedom of wonder, have been banished. Of course, wonder is costly. You couldn't incorporate it into a modern state because it is the antithesis of the anxiously worshipped security which is what a modern state is asked to give."

We need to strike a better balance between the world of facts and the world of wonder. Science itself arose as a new force on behalf of balance in human affairs. Before the rise of science, people lived in a world dominated by faith, but a faith often reduced to superstition and cant. The enlightened men and women of the Age of Reason saw science as a liberating force, while they perceived the Crown and the Church as bastions of reaction. The Enlightment, in the main, secured its goals. But we humans have a dreadful tendency to overshoot the mark. Once we get something going, we never know how to stop it until finally it too, through oversuccess, throws things out of balance. Having rejected blind faith, we put all our eggs in the one basket of rationality. What became noble was not blood, but reason.

As so often happens, the noble founder of a great house has many progeny, but few of these display the attributes of their mighty progenitor. Today, the distant descendants of noble reason are ever so many little thin-blooded facts, none of whom even remotely resemble the founder of their house. Like the Spanish Hapsburgs, they have intermarried so much over the years that the end of their line is a bunch of blooming idiots.

Despite this faltering heritage, the notion remains widespread that the quality of public policy depends almost exclusively on technical and economic analysis. Just try to fight a civic battle by asserting ethics in public policy. People feel embarrassed for you and they snicker at you behind your back. They don't want to hear you talk about the decent thing to do. They want to talk about the facts.

The trouble is that facts are for sale. You can buy any facts you want if you have the money to pay for them. Social scientists are capable of endlessly churning out facts made to order. This is readily seen in public opinion polls in which the same question phrased in two different ways can elicit opposing responses from the same person. "Facts are not the givens," says sociologist Ida Hoos. "Facts are gotten." So we must ask who is getting them, and for what purpose. Do the facts lead to decisions or do they merely justify them?

The taxpayers have footed the bills for countless numbers of social science research projects devoted to every conceivable topic, and the file cabinets and library shelves are groaning with the voluminous results; facts, facts, and more facts People are in need of housing, jobs, education, better nutrition and health care, and of a clean, healthy environment, and it looks to me as if all the millions of facts that have been generated in recent decades haven't moved us very far in meeting these needs. We'd rather study a problem than solve it. The study provides the illusion but not the reality of action.

So don't confuse me with the facts, man. The facts are just standing in the way.

Systems Never Do What They Are Set Up to Do — Thank Goodness!

In Gulliver's Travels, Jonathan Swift tells of a community in which "persons with very little smattering of Mathematicks" return home from their education to "put everything on a new foot." Every town is to have an academy:

> In these colleges, the Professors contrive new Rules and methods of Agriculture and Building, and new Instruments and Tools for all Trades and Manufactures, whereby, as they undertake, one Man shall do the Work of Ten; a Palace may be built in a Week, of Materials so durable as to last forever without repairing. All the Fruits of the Earth shall come to Maturity at Whatever Season we think fit to chuse, and increase a Hundred Fold more than they do at present; with innumerable other happy Proposals. The only Inconvenience is, that none of these Projects are yet brought to Perfection; and in the mean time, the whole Country lies miserably waste, the Houses in Ruins, and the people without Food or Cloths. By all which, instead of being discouraged, they are Fifty Times more violently bent upon prosecuting their Schemes, driven equally on by Hope and Despair.

Swift's satire of academic planning, uptopian schemes, and the methods used in the social sciences was prescient. He saw what was coming and put his finger precisely on its flaws. We need a Swift today to satirize the decline and fall of all these Rules and Methods and Instruments and Tools. Only a satirist could truly capture the massive Inconvenience wrought by these innumerable happy Proposals.

The modern experiment to govern humanity through scientific methods has failed. That is the long and short of it. Science was devised to learn truths about the physical world, and these truths, once discerned, may indeed alter our perceptions about ourselves, others, and the universe. These perceptions may also alter our social relationships, but that is a far cry from governing them. Science is no tool for administering society. Human beings are contrary and essentially ungovernable. We are messy, wicked, and full of surprises and delights, qualities that baffle and evade poor science. To me, the term social science is a contradiction; science and society don't mix very well. Oh, sure, the social sciences can count heads and, based on that, issue pieces of paper called checks, but that is about the extent of it. I love true science, and I hate to see it debased and twisted into purposes for which it was never intended.

Here is how this debased science is supposed to work. It assumes, first of all, that people are purely rational beings, a proposition so wrong-headed that even a Neanderthal would have seen through it. Nevertheless, we press on with this assumption and when a problem arises we set out to fix it using the rational model. First we collect all available evidence so we can establish the facts. Then we analyze the facts to establish findings. Based on the findings, we devise a plan. To carry out the plan, we devise a system. If the system is put in place permanently, we call it an institution. To fulfill its responsibility, this institution must be vested with formal authority, and so we pass laws or adopt regulations that permit the imposition of sanctions or penalties, if necessary, to secure compliance with the plan. Eminent and qualified persons are appointed to head the institution and to administer the laws and regulations; these persons are called administrators. Because the plan is often very complicated, administrators are authorized to employ other individuals to assist them. Because administrators are expected to conduct the plan in a manner that is both scientific and efficient, they employ persons possessing technical training or education. Such persons are called specialists.

What I have described here, in grossly simple fashion, is the method usually employed by society to attack social problems. This method is derived from science and thus it should be elegantly logical, methodical, and orderly. It aspires to be all these things, and yet it fails miserably. If scientific government worked, we would all be living in paradise because we have the finest technical bureaucracies money can buy. What these big systems really do is generate paper flow and issue contracts and grants. A report here, a report there. A billion dollars here, a billion dollars there. Here a damn. There a dam. Everywhere a damned dam. Bricks and mortar. Concrete and pavement. Machines and equipment. But reports and money and buildings and tools do not necessarily create housing, energy, health care, education, or welfare. We used to think they did, but we were wrong. How did we fall into such error?

Although the technical hierarchies we call bureaucracies are supposed to embody the best in scientific planning and management, little about them is logical or orderly outside of the organization charts, and sometimes even the organization charts are a form of lunacy. Visit a bureaucracy some day. See if you can sense the frenetic aimlessness as you enter the building. Then try to find your way around. Note that the complicated room numbering system makes no sense. If you are a Very Important Person, the bureaucrat whom you are visiting will dispatch a secretary to meet you at the entrance and guide you to the proper office; otherwise, you might get lost. Stroll down the corridors. If you listen carefully, you will hear muted sounds of warfare. Around the water fountain, you can pick up the whispered account of feuds and purges, rebellions and oppressions. The whole place is riddled with emotion and conflict. Whatever has become of cool, calm, dispassionate science?

Robert S. Hutchings, my boss when I worked in government years ago, is a fine writer who taught me the rule that bad copy can never be rescued. The only thing that you can do with bad copy is toss it out and start fresh with something that is clear, simple, honest, and sensible. But technocracy flees from anything that is clear, simple, honest, and sensible.

I suppose technocrats think it might be contagious. I sometimes think of Hutchings's Rule when I stroll down the corridors of a bureaucracy. I hear all those typewriters clattering away at what is almost certain to be fundamentally bad copy. I see all those file cabinets bulging with fundamentally bad copy, and all those photocopiers spewing out thousands of sheets of fundamentally bad copy. I think of all those bureaucrats spending sleepless nights and getting ulcers because they have to wrestle with ton after ton of fundamentally bad copy.

Stafford Beer, the British systems analyst, says that "Systems never do what they are set up to do. Systems do whatever it is they do." Beer asserts that we never look at what systems really do. Maybe we cannot bear to look. If a system is performing badly, we never dismantle it. We try to buck it up. If one system does not work, we establish another. If the law we passed does not secure the desired result, we pass another, this one with longer, more complex provisions and more stringent penalties. If a public agency does not fulfill its responsibilities, we grant it more authority, more money, more staff, and assume that will do the trick. But what happens when we run out of tricks? What happens when technique itself is exhausted?

Rather than reduce the number of systems, we much prefer to establish new ones. In the beginning, we are always supremely confident that the new system will do the job. Then as time passes, we watch in horror and amazement as the new system begins to neglect or even subvert the social goal it was established to serve. This happens time and again, but each time it does we act as if it were a totally unexpected assault upon our innocence.

A good example is utility regulation. At the beginning of our history we set up state legislatures for the purpose of representing the people and promoting the public interest. But in the nineteenth century along came the railroads, which represented an alliance between wealth and technology, and virtually every state legislature was bribed into submission by the robber barons that owned them. As abuses grew, so did demands for reform. After great effort by an aroused citizenry, a new system was put into place to solve this problem. This new system was the regulatory commission, and it was believed that such commissions, because they were independent of the venal legislatures, would set high standards of public service. But when a little time elapsed and a lot of money changed hands, the regulatory commissions themselves fell prey to the illicit charms of the regulated interests. Most wound up as little more than tax-supported apologists for the interests they were supposed to regulate.

The Romans had a proverb: "Who is to regulate the regulators?" How do systems get so far off the track? It begins the minute a new system is installed. The very first thing that happens is that some people get hired. At exactly this point, certain institutional imperatives begin to take over that quickly outmaneuver the stated altruistic purpose of the system. First of all, in our society, jobs represent material security as well as sources of self-esteem. If nothing better comes along, employees want to hang onto their jobs until death or retirement, whichever comes first.

Just as naturally, employees continually press for more pay and higher status. This, too, is a fact of life, at least in America where capitalism teaches us to constantly expect more. Now the second institutional imperative comes into play: The system must keep expanding. If the people in the system are to make more money and achieve higher status, then the budget must increase and the organization must grow in size.

The Congress, the state legislature, or the city council must be persuaded to pay the ever-growing costs. How is this achieved? The system has a job to do, handed it by the public. But it fails to do that job. You might think that its failure to perform would lead to the system's demise, that its mandate and appropriations would be withdrawn. But this almost never happens. Instead, the system goes back to Congress, the state legislature, or the city council and demonstrates conclusively that it lacks the authority or the money or the staff needed to do its job. They can usually sell this case for a very good reason: It is true.

The dynamics of industrialism, up to now at least, produce an ever-expanding complexity. The problem is always growing bigger and moving faster than attempts to solve it. Government agencies given the job of ameliorating industrialism's ill effects must always play catch-up ball. For example, new toxic substances are being devised and released into the air and water faster than the Environmental Protection Agency can detect or control them. The complex, dynamic reality of industrialism does not lend itself to control by public authority. This is the real dilemma we face, and while we bemoan big government, we must remember that it was induced by the abuses of big business. From the Interstate Commerce Commission to the Food and Drug Administration to the Securities and Exchange Commission to the Consumer Product Safety Commission, the struggle of government to get on top of problems produced by industrialism has been characterized by efforts to mirror and thereby to master the complexity of industrialism. Every one of these agencies was established to meet a clear and present threat to public welfare and every one of them was established with massive public support. To pull the plug now on these efforts would leave the same basic problem—the nature of industrialism—unresolved. Small government cannot defend us against the abuses of big business. And big business cannot or will not curb its abuses or reform itself. So long as big business exists, I am afraid we have no choice but to leave big government in place to provide us some defense.

While I can swallow this in theory, I must admit I have a hard time swallowing it in reality since bigness itself is the problem. When you take outsized scale and add to it the faulty assumptions of government by science, you have created an unmanageable mess. Accountability, the very essence of free government, is reduced to a blur. You can never get a straight answer out of a bureaucracy. When a problem surfaces, there is always somebody else, up or down the line, who is to blame. It is the person in contracts or in programs review or in policy evaluation whom you ought to tackle. It is never the person to whom you are talking.

This absence of accountability allows the political system to do cruel and stupid things that human beings (except for the criminally insane) would never do in their private capacity. A man who is devoted to his wife, loves his children, and would never think of kicking his dog, will, in his official capacity, sign an order taking food out of the mouths of the hungry poor. And he does not feel accountable when he does it; he is just doing his job.

Large institutions possess no memory and this too helps them to evade accountability. For years, heads of the Federal Aviation Agency publicly swore that they would never allow noisy jet aircraft to use National Airport, which is located close to residential areas in downtown Washington. But when jets started flying into National Airport, they flew with the blessings of the FAA. The administrators who had made the promises to the citizens had long since moved on. The agency itself had totally erased the memory of the commitment that had been made. Because big institutions cannot remember, they cannot be called into account. Since they cannot be called to account, they can behave dishonorably without a twinge of conscience.

The best way to appreciate the workings of large bureaucracies is to take one on in a fight. The experience can be exhausting. Everything is in flux. Titles and official responsibilities of agency employees continually change. The person you dealt with last month has been reassigned. The person you are dealing with now is new to the job and doesn't know beans about it, and you are supposed to be polite and patient while he learns the ropes. Internal organization constantly shifts. Yesterday's division of management information is today's bureau of program management. They expanded overnight.

Offices are constantly being moved from one location to another. The records you require are either about to be packed, already packed, or not yet unpacked. Even the phone numbers don't remain the same for long. Entire new phone systems, with special codes and hard-to-obtain special directories, appear frequently to block any simple outside inquiries.

The confusion within a system is more than matched by the confusion that exists between systems. Incoherence is the order of the day. However, life is experienced as a whole. If your toe aches and you chop it off to be rid of the pain, your entire system will be affected and walking will never again be the same. Specialized systems ignore this basic truth. In the guise of science, they attack some portion of society's problems without regard to the well-being of the whole. Nowadays, irony of ironies, such assaults are conducted in the name of "comprehensive planning." But there is no such thing. It is a fraud. For example, health plans do not look at transportation systems and transportation systems do not look at health plans. Yet automobile pollution and automobile accidents are probably one of the largest causes of health problems in the country.

If you go to the Department of Energy to ask what effects on employment various energy scenarios will have (I have actually done this), they cannot tell you. They will inform you haughtily that they are the Energy Department, not the Labor Department. If you go to the Department of Labor to find this information (I have done this too), they will tell you to buzz off because they are the Labor Department, not the Energy Department.

Both departments are spending many millions of dollars on scientific and social research but they do not spend one dime on research examining the relationships between their areas of responsibility, even though it is increasingly clear that this is where the key questions now reside. As a result, these questions never get asked, officially at least. This conceptual fragmentation makes the achievement of any overview impossible, and without an overview how can we tell where we are headed? But maybe we should not deplore this apparent aimlessness too much. Maybe big systems cannot, should not, point the way for us. Maybe they cannot take us where we want to go.

If big systems actually worked well, we would probably fall under their control even more than we have at present. An inefficient tyranny is to be preferred over an efficient one. So long as we retain our political freedom it will ensure enough dissent and diversity to evade the sluggish pace of bigness. Maybe we should thank our lucky stars that big systems get mired down in their own gigantic complexity. This fatal flaw may provide the best insurance yet for the continuation of political freedom in the industrial order.

Where Are the Robber Barons Now That We Really Need Them?

We all know that power can be used for evil purposes, but shouldn't the nature of power also include the capacity to serve good purposes, to create useful or beautiful things? Otherwise, why do we permit power to exist in human communities?

Power is, of course, a fact of life. Some people have it and some people don't. Actually, most people don't, or so they will tell you if you ask them. Most people feel that power is a possession of a privileged few and that it is used far more often to harm the interests of ordinary people than to benefit them. So, I think it is fair to ask, why don't most people get together and act to curb or abolish power?

One reason they don't is that they lack the means to convene. Convening takes leadership and leaders must have power or they cannot lead. And if such a convening occurred, what would it do? How would it operate? What power would it use to abolish power?

Even the most violent revolutions, those that succeeded most thoroughly in demolishing the old power structure (e.g., the French and Russian revolutions), did not succeed in eradicating power as such. Power quickly reappeared on the scene and in forms, as luck would have it, even uglier and more brutal than before.

So back to my original question: If we can't escape the presence of power in human communities, can't we at least expect that it sometimes be applied to positive effect? Have we been so depressed and disappointed by the abuse of power that we have forgotten that it can also be used for good? Let's take one example. I love railroads. They provide, or used to provide, efficient, safe, convenient transportation. Relative to other modes of transportation, they conserve energy and do little damage to the environment. Nothing would make me happier than to see the nation's rail system restored to its former glory. I can think of few things that would benefit the general public more. Thus, it is fair to ask: Where did the railroads come from? Who had the power to generate this good thing?

Doubtless the robber barons responsible for building the

railroads were a gang of thieves who all deserved to hang, but they did create the railroads, and as I read American history, it seems that the railroads brought more good than harm to the country. Yes, some people were harmed by the coming of the rails, American Indians, for example; and the environmentalists of the day opposed railroads because they were noisy, smoky, and ruined the scenery. But you have to give the devil his due. The robber barons wrought real change, took real risks, and often suffered real losses. Some of them, having made and lost several fortunes, died in abject poverty. But with their soiled and grasping hands, the robber barons set the mighty rails in place.

Today's corporate barons are only pale copies of their lusty, raffish, and creative predecessors. They may occupy big, fancy offices and draw huge salaries, but they are no match for the free-wheeling builders who founded the great corporations. They lack the raw energy, the unbounded confidence and optimism, and the guts of the robber barons, though some of them may equal their predecessors in the extent of their greed and criminality. We have seen this venal side of modern industrialists in the brutality of corporate mergers and in the bribery plots perpetrated by some of America's largest corporations.

Corporate power in America has become bureaucratized along with everything else. It has lost the imagination and creative potency that once provided a counterweight to its brutal and exploitative aspects and the best excuse for its existence. Today's corporate chieftains are often accountants who have gotten to the top by never rocking the boat. If they had behaved like Commodore Vanderbilt or Diamond Jim Brady, they would have been fired a long time ago.

In the days of the robber barons, leaders could still lead. The institutions they created were new and small enough to be responsive to personal direction. When businesses are owned and controlled by individuals or by families, some real accountability to the customers exists. When I grew up there were two radio/television repairmen in our small town and they did good work at reasonable prices. They had to, for if they did poor work or overcharged, word would get around town quickly and they would lose their customers to repairmen in neighboring towns. More importantly, they felt a sense of responsibility to their fellow citizens. Today, if you live in a big city and your radio or television goes on the blink, you are horrified since you know that when you take it for repairs you are almost certain to be overcharged. You might as well throw it out and go buy a new one.

Fewer and fewer businesses are owned, however, by individuals and families. Businesses that succeed get bought up by larger concerns or grow large enough to go public. Grandmaw Jones' Pie Company no longer belongs to Grandmaw Jones. She sold it for a bundle to Global Pastries, a division of International Polyethylene, Inc., and moved to her condominium in Florida. The pies they make are lousy, but so what? They sell by the zillion from coast to coast.

Of course, a lot of businesses owned by individuals or families get run out of business by bigger companies. The pretty little sandwich shop on the corner where you used to get a terrific egg salad is long since gone. Not to worry, though. There's a fast-food joint in the same location where you can drive right up to the window and take your pick of their hamburgers, fried chicken, and pizza.

Personal control of business has been replaced by scientific management. Scientific management means that you sell lousy pies but you make a lot of money. It also means you introduce a lot of technological complexity and centralized control to the business. When this happens, bureaucracy develops and begins to take over, drastically reducing the ability of the people "in charge" to run things. Pretty soon the business leaders begin to resemble their counterparts in public bureaucracies The bosses are not bosses at all, but mere front men for the bureaucratic imperatives of the institution.

The men who built the railroads may have been petty tyrants, but at least they <u>built</u> something good! They were entrepreneurs on a grand scale, not bureaucrats and accountants. They had a clear eye for the main chance and the vision to seize it. They had the ability to discern which direction history was headed. Go west, young man. Today's corporate leaders, for the most part, lack the ability to see which direction history is headed. In fact, they are afraid to take a peep! They want it to be 1951 all over again.

Meanwhile, their so-called power is used for such retrograde activities as the manufacture of potato chips that stack. Or worse, their power is used for purely destructive purposes like the building of bigger and better bombs. Wouldn't you rather have business restore the railroads than make bombs? I would, and they can make all the money they want so long as train service is improved.

Not only did the robber barons build railroads, they did it with a certain elan that I find more attractive than the bland, bureaucratic mode of today's corporate leaders. The robber barons were indeed sinners, but their sins were human, not bureaucratic. They were vivid personalities with quirks and foibles that are memorable still. When they were around you knew whom to hate. J. P. Morgan with his red, bulbous nose, his flinty little ryes and his huge walrus mustache was easy to recognize and easy to hate. But today who even knows the names of the gray-faced characters who run the massive trusts he organized?

The robber barons laid the tracks not only for the railroads, but for the vast industrial system that still delivers life's basic necessities to our doors. This system, while it is aging and becoming increasingly vulnerable, still continues to work Until something better comes along, we can't afford to knock it altogether. No matter what you think of it, you have to admit that America's industrial plant represents a tremendous achievement by people in the past. Imagine, they hooked practically every home in America with little wires that brought electricity and little pipes that brought water right into the kitchen! As a child and as a young woman, my grandmother, had to carry water from a well for domestic purposes. She did it day after day, year after year, and she tells me it was no fun. She thinks it's awfully convenient to turn a faucet and have hot water pour out of it. Maybe we owe a bit of thanks to those old crooks who put the deal together.

However, it disturbs me to think that the industrial system we rely on is not being renewed and strengthened. The railroads are about to fall apart. And in all the vast bureaucracy now running the railroads, there is probably not one person with the courage and vigor to restore them. America's managerial class is content to exercise its stock options, but not its imagination and initiative. In the long run this lassitude may be beneficial since the imagination and initiative of the managerial class once aroused is deployed in exactly the wrong direction, producing such disasters as the Vietnam War and nuclear power. I suspect that the robber barons, if they were still around running things, would have pulled out of Vietnam and out of nuclear power when the first negative feedback began appearing. They may have been crooks, but they had nothing if not guts. If the emperor was wearing no clothes, they wouldn't have hesitated to tell him so. They wouldn't have been caught unaware by the energy crisis. By this time they might have bought and sold the sun a hundred times over, but the nation might have a lot of solar technology in place and working.

What about us? Are we going to be allowed to sit back effortlessly while the fruits of mass production roll in and in and in? This can't go on forever for, as Professor Barry Commoner, the scientist and environmentalist, has reminded us, there is no such thing as a free lunch. We have to pay up sometime. Today's products reflect the inspiration and dedication of an earlier generation of creators and the sweat of an earlier generation of workers. We are still living off the tinkerers, the entrepreneurs, and the laborers who built the mighty machine, set it in place, and got it going. But what are we doing in return? What energy are we investing so that future generations can live off us for a while as they struggle to make their own way in the world? We were given a gift. Shouldn't we pass one on?

I should like to put this question to the managerial class in America: What leadership is being provided by the technocratic elite to justify their privileged existence?

In fairness, I should observe that there is a good reason that the technocratic elite fails as leaders: The nature of technocracy itself prohibits the rise of leadership. Any system that exalts clerks over innovators deserves to come crashing down. The fragmentation of authority in large organizations makes for timid managers. The breakdown of authority ties their hands; they cannot fire or discipline subordinates. They don't want to be sued, they don't want to be hassled, and they don't want to be disliked. So, in their hearts, the technocratic leaders of today s industries have lost their will and confidence to lead. If it weren't considered unmanly to show feelings, you wouldn't be able to hear anything in corporate boardrooms except the sound of sobs.

What would Diamond Jim Brady and his partners in crime think of the sorry condition of business leadership? If we could resurrect them, could they do any better? I expect the answer is probably not; not if we stuck them in technocracy and expected them to work their wily schemes from there. Technocracy would probably defeat even Diamond Jim. Oh, he personally would come out on top. Maybe he wouldn't be able to build or even restore a railroad, but he'd probably wind up as chief of the bureau of personnel management. You can t keep a good man down!

I Don't Know Much about Science, But I Know What I Like

Commenting disparagingly on the notion of human progress, D. H. Lawrence once observed that people were still washing dishes by hand after thousands of years of civilization. Today, of course, science has relieved us of this onerous chore by providing the dishwasher. Thanks to science, maybe we do progress after all.

On the other hand, I have one of these machines and I am sorry to say that there are some drawbacks involved in using it. I practically have to wash really dirty dishes before I put them in; otherwise, they come out still dirty. Badly soiled pots and pans have to be scrubbed hard by hand, just as the peasants of ancient Egypt did it in the time of the pharoahs. Moreover, I spend a lot of time fitting in every utensil I can so that no hot water, soap, or electricity is wasted. This little exercise in conservation can develop into a game: How can I make room for that extra cup or bowl?

I have to be careful how I fit things in or glasses will knock against each other and come out chipped or broken. I must not place plastic or wooden items in the lower half of the dishwasher because they might melt or burn. And I must remember never, never to put good crystal or china in the machine because they are too expensive to replace if it damages them. Finally, when I turn on the machine, I have to leave the kitchen and close the door because the noise is so loud it gets on my nerves.

Here I am washing my dishes in the wonderful new way prescribed by science and it seems to be more tedious and time-consuming than the old way. Have I been fooled? Have technologists fooled themselves? Was D. H. Lawrence right to sneer at the idea of progress? What happened to the beautiful promise of science that stirred so many fine eighteenth and nineteenth minds?

Along with everything else on God's green earth, science has been industrialized. The systematic search for truth has become the systematic search for profit. The golden goose has been automated and put to work on the assembly line. Cheese in spray cans is what it's all about. A long shelf life for groceries has been secured at the cost of life for people. We live in a land where even hair dryers can give you cancer.

Pure science (if indeed it ever existed) has gone the way of the dodo. Maybe there are still a few genteel scientists puttering around with pure science in the privacy of their own laboratories. Or maybe some perverse, iconoclastic academics are pursuing pure science in the privacy of their minds. But there can't be very many of them, otherwise, we'd be getting better quality science. Skylab might not have fallen. Swine flu vaccine might not have spread swine flu. Pesticides might not be creating superpests and rendering crops more, not less, vulnerable.

If there are still some scientists doing research free of industrialism's greedy grasp, they should be placed immediately under the protection of the Endangered Species Act. Though their heads may be buried in the sand when it comes to the social consequences of their work, I would not deny them their sacred right to free inquiry for one moment. No path of theoretical exploration should be cut off. However, once any exploration poses significant social costs, benefits, or dangers then, of course, political processes should be brought into play. But that comes later. In its creative, theoretical stages, science is as pure, I suppose, as it is ever going to be. There it ought to be left alone.

My hackles do rise though, when the mandarins of science policy enter the picture. Although they may once have been practitioners of pure science, and maybe even distinguished at it, the members of this fraternity long ago traded the search for truth for the pursuit of power. These fellows want to have their cake and eat it too. They expect to be treated reverentially as the intellectual descendants of Copernicus, Galileo, and Newton, and they also expect presidents and politicians to do their bidding. Their psychological hankering is for the exercise of power without the nuisance of accountability.

Unless they are chief executives of multinational corporations (or directors of research at the least), the science policy mandarins do not work for industry, not directly. They are distinguished professors and presidents of prestigious consulting firms. They are chairmen and members of presidential commissions on which they serve generously for no pay. Grubby commercial considerations are the furthest thing from their minds, or so they will tell you if you have the effrontery to ask them about their relationship to industry But they like to live well and their grants and contracts have to come from somewhere. Business is business.

If Professor X holds a dozen corporate directorships, we are not supposed to infer that these lucrative affiliations just might influence his professional judgments. If Doctor Y gives expert testimoney in a suit brought against the oil companies by the government, we are not supposed to ask if his long and highly remunerative consulting relationship with these same companies just might influence his testimony. The reason we are not supposed to question these relationships is that both gentlemen have donned the sacred robes worn by experts. They are wanted not for their influence, but for their expertise. And expertise, as we all know, is as pure as the driven snow.

When it comes to the debasing of science, however, it should be said that money is not the root of all evil. Pride plays a part that is nearly as large. Vested intellectual interests can be as corrupting as vested economic interests, and they are harder to trace. No scientist is truly capable of entirely divorcing his ego from his work; that just isn't humanly possible. Scientists want to <u>succeed</u> in their work, so naturally they address problems they think they can solve. Right here they get into deep trouble and a fundamental bias creeps in: Scientists are <u>pro-solution</u>, that is, <u>pro-technology.</u> Scientists like to fix things and they like to do it with machines. In itself this psychological predisposition may be useful or even commendable, but it certainly is not objective. What about all the things that can't be fixed by machines but require some form of social action?

Take cancer, for example. The science policy mandarins have

successfully urged us time and again to invest billions of dollars in research to cure cancer, that is, to isolate some virus that causes it. But for decades evidence has been piling up that strongly indicates that the cancer epidemic is attributable to industrial processes (e.g., chemical additives in food), environmental pollution, and smoking. With rare, commendable exceptions, scientists have not been in the forefront of attacks on these problems. Twelve years ago, I was active in the citizens' movement for clean air and I can tell you first-hand that the Boy Scouts were way ahead of the medical profession in recognizing air pollution as a threat to public health. Shouldn't physicians "be prepared" at least as well as the Boy Scouts?

The thing is, scientists can isolate a virus, but they cannot direct a campaign to correct the abuses of industrialism. They have neither the talent, the temperament, nor the training for such work and we should not expect them to do it. Social problems are hard to fix, if indeed they can be fixed at all. Remember, scientists are temperamentally addicted to solutions. Professor Gerald Holton, the Harvard physicist, states, "The main charm of work in a physical or biological science is that it ideally permits one to formulate statements of simple lawfulness that are the very opposite of the complexity characterizing most social questions and interactions." Drawing on a number of studies examining the psychology of scientists, Holton suggests that persons attracted to science as a profession are seeking a safe refuge from the irreducible complexity of reality.

According to Holton, scientists as a type dislike interpersonal contact because complex human emotions are not subject to control, that is, to solution. The scientist, as Holton sees it, is "preoccupied with control, with the need for order and structure that extends from regularity of schedule to ready acceptance of authority outside his own field of expertise." Now the qualities of leadership, as I understand them, scarcely consist of dislike of other people, fear of emotions, a preoccupation with control, and a complaisant submission to the authority of others. This sounds to me like the anti-politician, which is, I guess, what the mandarins of science policy are.

Politicians, after all, are subject to some rudimentary forms of accountability. Even the worst and most corrupt of them occasionally have to press the flesh of some ordinary people. But the mandarins of science policy garbed in their sacred robes of expertise, never have to mix with their inferiors.

I do not mean to suggest that the mandarins are cold to those in want or insensitive to human suffering. Many, if not most of them, are not. Indeed, politically, a lot of the mandarins are liberals of the bleeding-heart variety. They shed bigger tears than anybody for the poor and disadvantaged. It's just that they blithely go off and concoct solutions for the poor and disadvantaged without ever once thinking that the poor and disadvantaged might have something themselves to say about what ails them and what might be done to relieve them. The lack of public participation in science policy is virtually total, even though much of the population is deeply affected by decisions about what technologies are developed or subsidized and even though taxpayers pay the bill. We are excluded from policies on toxic wastes, radiation, nutritional values of foods, and other concerns that directly affect our lives. Science policy, like economic, foreign, and military policies, has been largely roped off from the public and declared the province of experts.

Having myself a certain fondness for simple, sometimes facetious solutions, I have a proposal that would remedy this omission: Every time a science policy mandarin is appointed to some official policy review board, study commission, or advisory committee, there should also be appointed, at random, a poor, black, pregnant, unwed teenage girl. Her appointment would be justified on the basis that the social data she embodies is so <u>different</u> from the data he contributes that it would be intellectually dishonest not to consult it. Count the differences between them. She is black; he is white. She is young; he is middle-aged or old. She is unwed; he is married. She is unemployed; he enjoys academic tenure, consulting fees, and corporate directorships. She is poor; he is affluent. She lives in the ghetto; he lives in the suburbs. She is unknown and unnoticed; he is respected, even renowned. She is worried and afraid; he looks to the future with complacency She is going to have a baby; he cannot have a baby even if he lives a thousand years

Now, what enables him with his view of the world to make policy that fits her? Might not we justifiably turn the whole thing around and decree that, in the future, she will design the policies that affect him? If in the design of public policy we are going to heed only one view of the world, then should we not—in the name of justice—at least alternate the world views once in a while, just to air out the closets of thought?

Furthermore, haven't those sacred robes of expertise grown tattered and soiled through overuse? What does this vaunted objectivity consist of anyway? For example, is there anyone alive who thinks there are nuclear physicists still capable of complete objectivity about nuclear power? Most nuclear physicists, of course, favor it. In one way or another, they derive their livelihood from it. But they also have an emotional investment in the technology. It is their pride and joy. It is their solution to a painfully complex human need. After the accident at Three Mile Island, Harold Lewis, a physicist at the University of California at Santa Barbara, was quoted as saying, "There has always been this feeling that nuclear power is fragile, that it is so complex, so beautiful, so delicate that it has to be protected from people who don't understand it." There they are again, the hoi polloi, messing up the scientists' beautiful dream of cheap, boundless energy for all time to come.

The people, however, have noticed that this dream is tarnishing. Is the pride of the majority of nuclear physicists in nuclear power consistent with objectivity? Can we rely on persons so emotionally involved with the technology to make responsible judgments about its safety and reliability? Some physicists, of course, are outright opponents of the technology. In fact, they are its most effective critics. Is this outright opposition objectivity? And then, I suppose, a handful of physicists are honestly confused about whether or not nuclear power is a good idea. Does their confusion make for objectivity?

An important adjunct to the claim of objectivity is the claim that technology is neutral. This just isn't so. To deploy a technology throughout society is to make a series of political decisions and economic commitments. As Harvey Wheeler of the Center for the Study of Democratic Institutions in Santa Barbara, California, has put it, "Science has become society's legislature. That is the general political implication of the scientific revolution." The introduction of solar energy into society, for example, will either destroy or create jobs, depending on the form the technology takes. It will either concentrate or redistribute income and wealth. It will either centralize or decentralize human settlements. It will primarily serve the interests of big corporations or of small businesses and consumers. It will enhance or degrade the environment. But however the technology develops, its effects will not be neutral.

Because technology has often been introduced with little awareness of its social impacts, it has sometimes created terrible problems of ethical choice. Take kidney dialysis machines, for instance. Who gets access to them? Everyone who needs one? Society can afford to produce only a few such high-cost items. Since it is obvious that not everyone who needs access to expensive health care technologies can have it—we are not even providing sufficient access to inexpensive health care—we create an ethical dilemma by devising such technology. Because the conflict over access to such technologies is nearly always resolved in favor of those who can afford it, such technology is biased, like everything else, in favor of the rich and powerful. Does this mean that we shouldn't manufacture kidney dialysis machines? Does this mean that science should be used to assist society in redistributing wealth so that access to technology, among other things, is more equitable? What has science got to do with the distribution of wealth, anyway? What Pandora's box of social issues do we open here? Aren't we getting in kind of deep?

Such problems will get worse before they get better. In biology, for example, technology is producing new social options of the most fundamental kind. Do we, or do we not, want to produce test-tube babies, postponement of death, mind control, genetic warfare, or new life forms? How do we decide? On technical grounds? On ethical grounds? On some new ground that is a combination of both? How in the name of heaven do we even begin to ascertain what that might be?

Scientists cannot go on forever having their cake and eating it too. They are going to have to assume moral responsibility for their work. They are going to have to admit the role of social values in science. Here, at long last, we come to the science I like. Advocacy, or public interest, science has sprung up in the last few years to challenge the complacency and hidden biases of industrialized science. The advocates are the first to admit that they have a point of view. They even call attention to it so that no one can be confused about their motivation. In effect, an advocacy scientist might announce in public: "Look, I have a bias. I favor clean air over dirty. I shall use my scientific training to attack dirty air and to promote clean air. I am a citizen as well as a scientist."

But, oh, how the mandarins of science object to the advocates' position! They see it as a betrayal of science, as heresy to the religion of quantification and objectivity. If the public interest scientists are heretics, they have at least the courage of their convictions. To perform public interest science requires, in nearly all cases, a financial sacrifice. Citizen and consumer groups, which are the clients of public interest scientists, can't afford to pay them much and in many cases the scientists work as unpaid volunteers. Therefore, the vested economic interest of the "advocacy" scientist to his or her client is slight. The "objective" scientist however, is usually paid very well indeed. I'm a simpleton, I know, to raise such a foolish question, but doesn't this suggest that "advocacy" scientists, working for little or no pay, are more capable of intellectual honesty than objective scientists who are well paid?

Of course, money is not the only issue. An advocacy scientist can be just as egotistically stubborn in his cause as any other scientist. It is possible sometimes to forego money, but foregoing pride is more difficult and rare. But it takes guts to practice public interest science, and isn't that proof of some devotion to the truth? It's easy to bow to the conventional wisdom. You get applauded and promoted for doing that. It's easy to join the crowd of senior colleagues who are certifying revealed knowledge yet again. The advocates, on the other hand, are outnumbered and outranked. They put their careers on the line. They take risks. To me, they resemble the courageous men and women who founded science, despite derision and persecution.

Public interest scientists make plain where their biases lie. They walk in and lay them on the table where all can see them. This simple, honest act causes the mandarins profound embarrassment for it suggests that all the other players in the game have their biases, too. Having revealed themselves, the advocates are then free to press on, making the best case they can, employing the methodology and tools of science to good effect. Then the search for truth can go forward unhindered and uncorrupted by hidden biases parading as objectivity.

Public interest science is the best thing science has going for it. By acknowledging the legitimate place of social value in science policy, the public interest scientists are laying the groundwork for a new science. This new science is built on the admission that science has been industrialized, and thus politicized. This new science acknowledges that all citizens are deeply affected by science policy decisions and that they have a right to a say in them. This new science attempts to address the moral and ethical dimensions of what science has done and might still do, and does not turn its back on these dimensions as if they did not exist. This new science is humble, not arrogant, and it reveres all the things science is not and can never be.

Whining Is Not Allowed

If you are an American citizen bothered by some government act or policy, take cheer. Under the Constitution, many courses of action are open to you. You can complain to public officials, write letters to the newspapers, or change the way you vote. You can consult friends and neighbors and if they agree with your complaint, you can organize a committee to take action. If you are really determined, you can ask your legislator to introduce new legislation and you can lobby for its passage. You can sue the bastards and obtain some ameliorative action through the courts. Or you can run for office youself, even the presidency.

You can perform wonders in American society as long as you are willing to become a volunteer. The catch, of course, is that volunteerism is hard work done for no pay. It's often taken as evidence of a weak mind or bleeding heart. Every serious course of action available to the citizen activist is laden with technical, legal, and logistical obstacles placed there by an establishment wary of direct citizen action. These obstacles keep most citizens obedient to and in fear of authority. The minority of citizens willing to run the gamut of obstacles find they risk their free time, their pocketbooks, and even their physical and mental health. Actually, voluntary action demands the very opposite of a weak mind or bleeding heart. You have to be determined, persistent, ingenious, and shrewd to succeed through voluntary action in America these days.

Let's take a common form of citizen participation, the public hearing. Now public hearings are fine, assuming that they are conducted in good faith and administered fairly. But this is the exception, not the rule. Things can go wrong with public hearings and often they do, sometimes by malicious design, sometimes by bureaucratic ineptitude.

Participation in public hearings on federal, regional, and state questions is usually restricted, in effect, to those who can afford the time and money to take part. You have to travel to Washington, D. C., or to a state capital. Besides, so many hearings are held on so many issues—a dozen a day in Washington alone—that citizens have a hard time keeping up, particularly since agencies like to spring them when they are least expected. Not everybody has a full-time lobbyist posted in the capital to watch out for his or her interests. And although government agencies do issue releases to the press, they do precious little else to alert citizens as to who might be affected by the hearings they are planning. Notifying affected parties (if they happen to be citizens or consumers) is left undone unless volunteers assume the task.

Even when citizens learn that a hearing will be held on some question of vital importance to them, they often face procedural impediments to their participation. Sometimes the hearing is a sham set up to mislead people or exhaust them while real decisions are made in the back room. Perhaps the hearing notice is incomplete or unclear. Poking through the gobbledygook, you cannot for the life of you discern what the hearing is really about! Perhaps access to data needed for any meaningful participation is costly, difficult, or even forbidden. Or the hearing is to be held at some inconvenient time or place. State highway commissions, for example, are infamous for staging their hearings in August when everyone is one vacation, or between Christmas and New Year's day.

Sometimes preliminary requirements for the hearing are irksome and unnecessarily demanding. You may have to sign up in advance, or you may have to indicate in advance what the thrust of your remarks will be. This helps the agency by alerting it to the nature of your concern and your opposition so it can prepare a rebuttal. You may have to provide ten copies of your testimony before you speak. This assumes you can type and have a photocopier handy.

Perhaps the agency will play favorites with the speaking order of those testifying. High-ranking officials get to go first because their time, presumably, is more valuable than that of ordinary citizens. Of course, as these officials sit there, they are drawing salaries while ordinary citizens, cooling their heels in the back of the hall, are there in their weak-minded capacity as volunteers.

Preparing for a hearing can be very time-consuming. Researching and writing testimony can take weeks. Organizing other citizens to take part can grow into a massive job. Then you have to get press coverage, for unless the question is a raging controversy, the media will probably ignore it. A volunteer must contact them and explain why the hearing is important. The press are fickle (there are so many things to cover) and in a sense they are lazy: They have to be hand-fed the analysis you have prepared to counter the agency's. The agency has credibility and usually you don't. This results in more hard work for the volunteer, but it won't do much good to turn out if the press isn't there to publicize your views. Citizen activists can always be dismissed as a small band of troublemakers and loonies by the decision-makers, but if dissident viewpoints are broadcast by the media, this put-down is less likely to stick. Besides, the agency is far more afraid of the press than of citizen critics. The spoon-feeding and hand-holding you have to devote to the press is worth the effort, even though media reporters are there on salary and you are not.

Even when hearings are conducted in good faith and the results are taken seriously, hearings remain inadequate devices for the full range of public participation. The area is too passive to allow creative initiative by interested citizens. People come to hearings to critique something they had no say in designing. Hearings provide no chance for partnership in creative design of public policy options. Of necessity, hearings consist of formal proceedings that must be highly structured and that allow little in the way of give and take.

Finally, after the hearing is over, it may take months, if not years, for the results to be known. Once they appear, you pore over the results trying to discover if your participation had any effect. You may be lucky to find any shred of evidence that you were present and counted.

Okay, so you rule out public hearings as an avenue of citizen participation in government or accept, reluctantly, their built-in limitations. What about other avenues? I hate to say so, but it turns out that every road is blocked in some way. Suppose you do the simplest thing: You go to the appropriate public officials demanding action. They may tell you not to worry, that there is no problem. That isn't air pollution you see; it's just mist blowing in from the sea. If they agree that a problem exists, they will assure you that it is being taken care of, or soon will be. Or they will weigh you down with reports and publications describing the immensity of the problem and their heroic efforts to deal with it. This device is called the data dump. Beware of it. You don't have to spend months (voluntarily) sifting through the documents to detect the faint odor of speciousness pervading them. Toss these documents into the garbage can and go back to demand a straight answer!

Public agencies grind out complex technical data by the ton, and as long as there is a photocopier and a clerk to operate it, officials will gladly bury you in information. What they will rarely provide is the critical, pertinent information you need. Of course, you could invoke the Freedom of Information Act to obtain the information you need, but that will probably divert you from your central purpose. Want a brand new fight? Try to make the Freedom of Information Act work. For that matter, try to save it from extinction.

No, you decide to press on, making use of the data you have secured. Some other poor sucker can tackle the government's improper withholding of information. Besides, you have finally discovered a public official who would love to help you. He would gladly act on your behalf, he says, but he lacks sufficient authority. If you go out and get a new law passed enabling him to do the right thing, he will quickly do it. Off you trudge, trusty volunteer that you are. You have become a lobbyist! Now, lobbying requires your frequent presence at city hall, the state capital, or in Washington, D. C. Soon you discover that the noble cause you have embraced has many enemies, most of them better funded, more experienced, and more powerful than you. They also are a mite less scrupulous.

(To you, of course, scruples are second nature.)

The worst part is that the laws that control lobbying discourage citizen activists from taking part. For example, a business is allowed to lobby to its heart's content and to deduct the costs as legitimate business expenses. But you are not a business and your costs cannot be deducted. Moreover, few people will contribute money to your lobbying effort because such contributions are not tax deductible. So you wind up absorbing many costs yourself. Maybe here you should abandon your original objective and take on the fight against business's unfair advantage in lobbying.

Luckily for you, however, justice makes one of her rare appearances and your elected representative comes through. A new law is passed! Jubilation! Now all you have to do is to get it enforced. This will be easy since you have already converted the appropriate public administrator to your cause. After all, he promised to act the minute the ink is dry on the new law. Oops! You find that he was transferred just last week and that his replacement used to be a lobbyist for the industry! Oh, come on now, chin up. You can always sue the new official and force him to act.

Here enters that resolute ally of the volunteer, the lawyer. Except for a handful of lawyers willing to volunteer their time and professional services, most lawyers insist on getting paid. And since the lawsuit you are bringing has many complex economic and technical dimensions, you need access to other professional expertise as well. Experts expect to get paid too. While you might succeed in wrangling free advice out of some of them, by and large you will have to pay for the information and analysis you need, and experts don't come cheap.

Meanwhile, printing and reproduction costs mount and your telephone bill has swollen to monumental proportions. Welcome to your new career as fund raiser! Begging money from other people is not as demeaning as you might think. When you have sacrificed your dignity once or twice, you begin to get the hang of it and soon you'll be hitting up everybody you know without even a trace of embarrassment. Remember, it's for the sacred cause. Of course, your contributors like to be remembered for their generosity. They rather think they have done you personally a favor and you have to play along with them. There is Mrs. Gotrocks, the widow of the fast-food tycoon, who once gave you $500 and maybe can be talked into it again. All you have to do is bow and scrape whenever she enters the room and flatter her every chance you get. Maybe there is some other tack you can take.

What about a mass media campaign? If you can get your story across through television and radio, the people no doubt will rally to your cause and force a solution. However, your cause is controversial and the media are afraid to cover it for fear of offending commercial sponsors. If you prepare an expensive public service campaign with your own spots and films (Caution: This involves fund raising), there is a chance you'll get it on the air. But competitors have safer, blander messages to convey, such as an antilitter campaign sponsored by the soft-drink and beer industries. So theirs is the free spot that makes it on the air. Maybe yours is broadcast at six o'clock on a Sunday morning. But, you protest, the airwaves belong to the people; they have a right and a need to hear about your cause. Your only recourse is to hire a lawyer to sue the station for keeping you off the air. Your original motivation for action now begins to fade while you are out trying to raise money to pay an attorney to sue a television station.

When you encounter any of these obstacles at any stage of your quest, don't whine—I'm sick to death of hearing myself do it. Consider your alternatives: Should you take on the fight to save the Freedom of Information Act, or should you join the battle against abuses of the Fairness Doctrine in broadcasting? What about the tax code that inhibits citizen lobbying? What about going directly to the issue of corporate responsibility itself through stockholder suits? The opportunities for engagement are endless and so are the opportunities for diversion. Should you go to law school? Should you get a Ph.D. in economics? Should you run for office or seek a political appointment? Should you deactivate?

Good Reasons Why You Can't Get a Grant

Suppose you—creative, altruistic, always energetic you—wake up some morning with a brilliant idea for an innovation, one that could benefit people for years to come. Your keen mind quickly deduces that the only thing separating your innovation from its immediate application to a grateful world is the money needed to demonstrate it. (Yes, a bug or two remain to be worked out. Sorry about that.)

Now if you or your mate or a close friend is independently wealthy and can pay for this work, you have it made. Congratulations and good luck! If this is not the case, you must march off to a bank or other financial institution in search of a loan to fund your work. Sad but true, you will find that very little capital is available to support innovation. Despite the myth of free enterprise, almost all capital is being gobbled up by big institutions who are powerful enough to get their hands on the money, but not creative or flexible enough to devise innovations.

When your banker has shown you the door, a light bulb in your brain turns on and you realize that the thing you need is a grant. After all, we live in an economy where billions of dollars are handed out every year by public agencies and private foundations to promote good causes and new, improved ways of doing things. Quite reasonably, you conclude that some minuscule portion of this money ought to head in your direction.

Suppose you come to me for advice on getting a grant. A look of pain would cross my face, but then I would smile sympathetically, offer you a cup of tea and warn you that the world is far more likely to kick innovators in the teeth than to support or reward them. But you, being brave and determined as well as gifted and virtuous, reject my advice out of hand and set out on your quest in search of a grant All right, go if you must, but please bear in mind these tips on grantsmanship.

First, you should know that good ideas are a dime a dozen and yours is no exception. There never has been a shortage of good ideas. People get them all the time. What is lacking is the luck, skill, patience, talent, and grit needed to actually bring a good idea to fruition. In nature, only one seed among many takes root, the others are gone with the wind. So it is with good ideas. Translating one into reality is exceedingly arduous and most people are not equal to the task. Now, you may honestly think you are equal to this work (I have already noted your many good qualities), and no one ought to deny you the opportunity to learn whether or not you are. Nor can anyone ever really tell you how long and hard is the road you have chosen, and even if they could, you wouldn't listen!

Many apparently good ideas are really nothing but hopeless causes dressed up in fine sentiments. Now some people get off by promoting hopeless causes, but I am not one of them. I like to win, no matter how distant or obscure my victory may be. So I soon learned, as a community organizer, not to spend time chasing impossible dreams. The possible dreams are hard enough, and after a while, even they will overwhelm you by the sheer extent of their numbers. Mere possibilities are floating around all over the place; if you want to win, you must identify which of them are inevitabilities, the sure bets, and lend yourself to their promotion.

All you need is the ability to detect the right idea at the right time. Take my word for it, you cannot then go wrong. The catch is, how do you acquire this intuitive ability? Some lucky few are those to whom God speaks directly; they have an inside track. If you are one of these, you certainly don't need my advice, but if you are not, you may have a problem. So far as I can see, the ability to detect inevitabilities is achieved only after a painful apprenticeship promoting hopeless causes and chasing after mere possibilities. Since you are only beginning your quest for a grant, it follows, by definition, that you are incapable of recognizing the right idea at the right time.

The system is a tough nut to crack. How do you know what innovations it will allow to break free from the pack and to soar off triumphantly? You haven't yet experienced the rejection and humiliation that will ultimately enable you to psych out the system and plot some cunning course of action whereby one of your good ideas takes hold and takes off; the right idea at last! Until then, your innovation is just another appealing, untested notion. Why don't you go back home, kid, where you belong?

Now for helpful tip number two. It will interest you to know that the people who hand out grants, the grants administrators, are well acquainted with the superabundance of unworkable good ideas and the scarcity of right ideas at the right time. Their awareness explains, in part, their systematic coolness to innovation. Indeed, such awareness is a useful ally to them in the service of their true function, which is not to give out grants, not, at least, to the likes of you. You must realize that you are the newest of many supplicants beseeching the grants administrators, a horde they are constantly struggling to evade. Furthermore, you must realize, that grants administrators, being human, have their own batch of good ideas they are aiming to fund. In order to evade such predators as you, and to protect their own pet ideas, grants administrators play for time. Time is on their side. While you are waiting for someone to give you a grant, you may tire or go bankrupt or starve to death and there will be one less predator outside their door. Your demise will only prove that you haven't got the gumption of a true, red-blooded American innovator. So much for the inevitability of your idea!

Don't forget that grants administrators are constantly on the receiving end of desperate, impassioned pleas and brazen, maniacal sales pitches intended to break them down and to wring a grant out of them by any means, fair or foul. To maintain simple human dignity they develop psychological defenses, just as surgeons learn to turn a deaf ear to the groans of the sick and dying. Though they may appear god-like to you, the anxious supplicant, grants administrators resemble divinities in one respect only: A profound reluctance to directly intervene in the natural order of things. Let nature take its course, they conclude with a sigh of relief. Only the hardiest of new ideas deserve to survive and they will survive anyway, with or without a grant.

This brings me to tip number three. You can t get a grant unless you already have a grant. If you have a grant, it is possible to obtain another, but if you don't have a grant, you can t have one. It's as simple as that, and if this rule sends you back to square one, so be it.

Having a grant, of course, is a credential that makes it easier to secure another. So it is in the interest of grants administrators to reduce the number of competitors with this credential, since there are already far too many applicants for the amount of money available. Besides making life a little easier for themselves, denying newcomers any funding increases the ability of grants administrators to fund their own pet projects.

Another reason that grants administrators will not give you your first grant is that they know that most of the money provided by the first grant will be speedily and ruthlessly applied to the grantee's real agenda, which is to secure the second grant and so on, _ad infinitum_. If they give you your first grant, what assurance do they have that you will not join the gang of grant addicts working to curb their discretionary power?

Now for my last tip. It's a biggie. You cannot get a grant to demonstrate an innovation until you have already successfully demonstrated it. Remember this: Nobody wants to fund a failure, but every grants administrator is eager to fund a success. Until your innovation is successfully demonstrated, how do they know it's not a failure? You have to provide proof in advance that your innovation works and you have to obtain this proof without a grant. Now how you do this is entirely up to you, although I can suggest the use of mirrors, black magic, or hallucinogenic drugs. Once you do this, however, you are sure to get a grant! In fact, if you pull this off, I may give you one myself.

Which Comes First, the Substance or the Process?

People in social movements usually share a vision of the future that is beautiful and inspiring, if somewhat fuzzy. When it comes to agreeing upon specific steps to reach their shared goals, however, they frequently have nasty fallings-out that impede their progress. This is somewhat silly, I know, particularly when everyone in the movement is nearly always sincere and dedicated. Nevertheless, details do have a way of disturbing the tranquillity of social movements and so they merit attention despite their triviality.

There are many explanations for the disputes that break out over specifics, but I would like to offer one that I find convincing, even if I did dream it up myself. This explanation focuses on the intense, but half hidden competition between substantive and political process goals. It's the old chicken and egg debate all over again: Should substantive or process goals come first?

Is it better to fight to improve a specific regulation, for example, or to improve access to the regulatory process? Or should you pursue both goals simultaneously? The easy answer to this latter question is yes, but in my experience, you have to be a superb juggler to do both and most people cannot keep that many balls in the air at once. So which comes first?

I am a process man myself and I am firmly convinced that process goals are equal in importance to substantive ones. (Okay, okay, so I _really_ believe they are superior to substantive goals.) I think process goals are generally neglected and deserve far more attention and support from citizen and public interest groups than they get.

After all, substantive victories for citizen groups are far more likely if the process is open and fair. Naturally, it is hard to imagine anyone quarreling with such an assertion, but the fact is that those concentrating on process reforms are a decided minority in social movements. If X, for example, is working to protect existing housing stock in older neighborhoods, X must keep narrowly focused on that substantive goal. Y, meanwhile, is working to protect the air and water quality that flows into the same community and Y must focus narrowly on that substantive goal. Now X and Y may never cross each other's path in their entire lifetime, even though both may be repeatedly tripping over the same process barriers. Meanwhile, Z has formed a committee to fight for process reforms, but few will join it. (Poor Z! I really identify with poor Z!) Both X and Y are much too busy to join; somehow they can't see the point of it when there is so much important legal and technical work to do.

I admit that, on the surface, substantive issues offer more attractive targets and goals than process issues do. They are more specific, visible, and definable than process issues. They come nicely boxed and wrapped in elegant quantifications. Inside are all kinds of things to play with, statistical data, weights, measures, that sort of thing. They provide a challenging game. For example, we want to know how much of some new chemical can safely be allowed in industrial processes. What laws apply to this decision? What standards should be issued? What do scientists know about the chemical and its effects? What are the facts?

We know (or think we know) how to deal with such questions far better than we know how to deal with imprecise, unmeasurable qualities such as decency or fairness. Process issues are hard to define. But substantive issues have their shortcomings as targets too. They tend to be narrowly focused and single purpose in character. They represent short-term determinations with little carry-over impact on the next policy decision. Process issues, on the other hand, have broad-range, long-term, pervasive impact.

No sort of reform is ever easy to secure, but the pursuit of substantive reforms offers the possibility of some discernible act or event that can be hailed as a victory, e.g., a legal or technical ruling. I appreciate the psychological significance of such victories. Those of us in the social change game need to win once in a while just to keep going. Process victories tend to be much less clear and certain.

Then again substantive fights involve some sizable drawbacks. The biggest of these is that, fighting on substantive grounds, you have to wade into technocracy up to your neck and this is enemy territory. In effect, you have to fight on the opposition's grounds of analysis and quantification. The glory of process issues is that they allow you to leap-frog over technocracy by asserting the primacy of ethics over technology, of common sense over specialization. The process reformer's stance is: "Damn the statistics! What is the decent think to do?" This simple question flies in the face of conventional wisdom, so it takes guts to ask it. But if you have the guts to ask it, certain tactical advantages accrue to you.

This question tends to clarify the debate, whereas technical analysis tends to complicate it. This question also helps to smoke out the specialists, forcing them to admit that they do not know everything, that, in effect, science can never replace common sense and social values in making political decisions. So asking what is the decent thing to do is asking a damned important question!

Still, over time, the impression has grown that substantive issues are somehow more important than process issues. Most people think that's where the action is. Certainly that's where the crowd gathers, and that's where the television cameras are aimed. Anything getting so much attention must be important. Who ever heard a major television network news show report on the status of a bill to improve public participation in government? The reporters are much too busy covering economic and energy policy to get around to such a minor topic as the perilous condition of citizenship. Besides, our educational system is busily churning out thousands of graduates in specialized fields—scientists, engineers, economists, and the like. They are ready, willing and anxious to work on substantive issues. But who is being trained to assert ethics in public policy? The principal contribution of American education to the promotion of ethics in public policy, so far as I can see, has been to produce a certain small number of drop-out theologians and unemployable art historians who get into community organizing and pick up the tattered banner of ethical standards to carry it bravely forward.

The contrast and competition between substantive and process goals is legitimate and would be entirely healthy if people on both sides would refrain from impugning each others' motives. People working on substantive issues are so intensely focused on their fight with technocracy that they fail to see the point of the process reformers' work. Because they are consumed by legal and technical specificities, they view process reformers as a little soft and mushy. Meanwhile, process reformers tend to see people working on substantive issues as just more technocrats doing their thing. We need to realize that we can't all have the same set of priorities and that passing judgment on each other is a drain, to say the least, on the spirit of fraternity that social movements require to stay alive.

The substantive work must be done, of course, and I am grateful that so many people have taken it on. But, by concentrating on substantive reforms to the neglect of process issues, we paint ourselves into a corner. Competition within the movement, not a bad thing in itself, becomes nasty when the social welfare advocates resent environmental activists, blue-collar organizers resent public interest lawyers, and so on. Everybody winds up competing for members, money, political support, the public's attention, and media exposure. Being human, we vest our particular causes with our own egos, thinking that what we are doing is the best, most important thing in the world.

Maybe we do have to psych ourselves up to make the effort and sacrifice that social change advocacy demands, but we don't need to continually dump on fellow advocates pursuing a different path. Process issues remind us that we are all in this thing together and help us to focus on across-the-board challenges and opportunities. I think that every so often substantive reformers ought to do a little process work, just to keep their hand in, so to speak. This might restore balance to their perspective and keep their skills in shape. Just as we need to exercise both mind and body, we need to command both substantive and process skills. Please don't recall that I started off this essay by observing that it probably can't be done. Just because something can't be done is no reason not to attempt it.

The Ego and I

Creation, in its boundless generosity, offers human beings a number of ways to transcend the bounds of self and experience the joys of selflessness. Among them are spirituality, intellectual wonder, aesthetic pleasure, natural beauty, and the act of love in all its many forms. Here too we find service to others and to the future. As good a path as any is the pursuit of the ideal human community.

People in social movements usually believe they are pursuing the ideal community in some way. So, naturally, social movements, being themselves a form of community, ought to embody as much of the ideal as is humanly possible to achieve. Sometimes I think they do; at their very best, social movements bring a little bit of heaven down to earth.

What are the characteristics of the ideal human community? I can only describe my vision of it. In my vision, it would be free and democratic. Voluntary agreement, not coercive force, would give it direction. It would be just, peaceful, self-sufficient, and beautiful. It would offer its members many opportunities for growth, self-expression, mutual support and affirmation. The community would be a creative one, always building for the greater good through release of the abundant energy and talent of its members. It would achieve unity while encouraging diversity.

Now social movements may not achieve all of these qualities all of the time, but it can be said that they aspire to them more faithfully and diligently than do, say, the business, the academic, or the political community. Then why do social movements keep folding? If they are so much nearer the ideal, why do they decline and die?

No consideration of social movements would be complete without a look at their darker side. Human failings invade social movements the minute they are launched; they seize control of crucial positions from which they can assail better human qualities at will. Ego—blessed, cursed ego—is the culprit.

Initially, I am always willing to attribute sincerity of motivation to almost everyone who enters a movement no matter why or how he or she joins. When the worst happens, as it sometimes does, and the movement is being hacked to death by its loudest adherents, I am still willing to find some sincerity in their motivation. I do this not because I am some relentless Pollyanna, but because I retain a sense of gratitude toward anyone who enters the fray or behalf of social change. I know that most people will never in their lives lift a finger to challenge authority or to fight injustice. For those willing to do so, I overlook, up to a point, the heavy load of ego demand some are prepared to dump on other people, including their own dear brothers and sisters in the cause.

People are attracted to social movements for a variety of reasons. Some treat this attraction like a religious calling; some treat it like a romantic passion. In either case, they expect a lot in return. This is only natural, but sometimes their needs are excessive, disguised, and ugly. Some people become psychological parasites on a movement, drawing strength from it rather than contributing to it. Some people are in desperate need of identity and expect the movement to provide it for them. Some are tragically, but inexorably, set on self-destruction of one kind or another. Frequently, they are all too willing to take the movement down with them.

Some people become extravagantly overcommitted to the cause, thereby causing imbalances in other parts of their lives. The mess that results they then conveniently label a sacrifice and a proof of dedication. It also serves as an excuse to blame others in the movement for not making an equal demonstration of total commitment.

Some people turn out to be motivated by deep wells of anger and bitterness. They wallow in disappointment and defeat. To these people, winning is unthinkable, even distasteful. They set up a self-fulfilling prophecy: To win is to sell out, that is, to lose.

Some possess wholly unrealistic expectations of what can be achieved. They grow furiously impatient when the going is slow, as it nearly always is. Some are, by nature, judgmental and intolerant. They collect grievances and spend most of their time looking for petty deviations from the true faith by their collaborators. When they encounter some presumed backsliding, they denounce it with a zest and fury never shown the common enemy.

Some people, for all their fine talk about sharing and community, are secretly harboring outsized ambitions for personal power and glory. But they are smart enough to know that one of the best ways to grab power is to wrap yourself in the cloak of selflessness and pretend that you have no interest in it whatsoever. If you wish to guard yourself against people involved in this form of power-tripping, there is a dead giveaway you should watch for. The ambitious are extremely competitive with others in the movement doing work <u>most similar to their own</u>. They can cheer on the volunteers, whose services pose no threat to them, but the collaborators working the same turf are viewed with cold, hostile suspicion. Should such collaborators score a breakthrough or victory, the glory-hungry will give themselves away by becoming physically or emotionally ill or aggressively destructive. In sorrow, I confess they would rather do in their perceived competitors than the common enemy.

These are the movement killers. They are always present in the social change community, just as they are in every other community. Why are they present? Maybe it's destiny's doing. Maybe we human beings aren't actually supposed to bring heaven to earth. So far as I can see, the purpose of life is to learn lessons, slowly to acquire wisdom, ultimately to reunite with perfection. Unending bliss in the here and now doesn't seem to be an option. So social movements, like all other living, growing things, must contain the seeds of their own destruction. The movement killers are just performing their natural functions. After all is said and done, they teach us many lessons, don't they? That the learning is painful can't be helped, I suppose. As the Buddhists say, "No pain, no gain." The clash of wills and temperaments inside the social change community is proof that it too is just another testing ground for human growth.

In this connection, I know whereof I speak. In my years as an organizer, a lot of people have slammed into me and I have slammed back. I have received my share of pain and, no doubt, I have given it to others. I have an ego too. I am fiercely committed to my own self-expression (read "ego") and woe betide all those who get in my way. I have been guilty of some, but not all, of the sins of pride herein described, but I have lived to tell the story. Much credit is due my opponents. Let's give the devil his due! I may still be reverberating in pain from the blows they have dealt me, but I am also still learning from them. To them, I owe my acute awareness of my own failings and limitations. Yes, I'm as egotistical as the next guy but, thanks to my enemies, I'm at least embarrassed by it. Just don't say I told you so. If I'm called up on charges of pride and egotism, I intend to plead self-defense.

Nobody's Perfect

Social movements are often assailed by their critics because their leaders fail to embody a pure expression of the values they are asserting. In the popular press, it boils down to whether or not you "like" Jane Fonda, Ralph Nader, or Gloria Steinem. This misses the point. It's also a cheap shot. Social movements are about values, about ideal qualities. Human beings are fallible; ideals are not. Mere mortals can't be expected to embody the ideal and, without exception, they do not.

Besides, social movements have many leaders of many different types. In my experience, most are highly evolved human beings possessing a greater sense of responsibility for the community as a whole than do most people. Most take this responsibility personally and seriously. To fulfill it, they shoulder a heavy burden for civic action. If some people weren't continually mending the social fabric, it would have long ago fallen into tatters since so many others are continually ripping it apart.

One of the principal joys of social action is the opportunity of association with persons of fine character. I know this sounds old-fashioned, like talk of ladies and gentlemen, good manners, civility, and other decrepit conceptions. But, bless their hearts, such virtues have not been totally eradicated. Surprisingly, social movements are one place to find them. Social movements are inhabited by classic good citizens of the type without whom the republic would fall in a minute. Their virtues are impressive and numerous: compassion, vision, integrity, fairness, and reliability, to name a few. They remind me of noble Romans of yore, but take my word for it, such people still exist. I am privileged to know a good number and I can tell you that they may be found in all parts of the land and in all races, creeds, and colors. Along with puppy dogs and the month of May, they offer abundant evidence that Creation is, after all, beneficent.

Rubbing shoulders with such people is a good way to build character. Not only are they earnestly attempting to live their lives according to high standards of citizenship, they will, if you persist in their company, expect you to do as much. This can sometimes be trying, of course, but it's nice to know that somebody is still out there holding aloft a banner of human conduct unbesmirched by raw egotism and greed for glory.

However, even this garden of social cooperation is marred by endless dispute over ideas, goals, policies, priorities, methods, strategies, and tactics. These disputes arise less out of excessive and misplaced pride than out of genuine differences between well-meaning people over what to do and how to do it. It's no secret that such disputes take place for they occur, by and large, in the open. They are so loud it's hard not to notice them.

Another, more subtle analysis of how these disputes originate can be presented. This analysis explores the inner workings of social movements, not from the point of view of intellectual and policy differences, but from the human dynamics involved. These sources of conflict are paid less attention. Indeed, they are often papered over in embarrassment. It's as if disputes based on high-minded thought and cool analysis are somehow more socially acceptable than those deriving from human interaction. Even we in social movements must cloak our motivations in the garb of reason. See how the debasement of science has contaminated us all?

These conflicts in pure thought and cool analysis are not the whole story, not even by half. People fight as much over where they sit as what they think. The struggles being waged on the surface—the substantive and policy fights—are so intense and unremitting that frequently it is hard to see behind them to find other deep roots of conflict. Besides, the public fights are bad enough for the image of social movements. If word got out that social activists are not, after all, one big happy family, it might lend aid and comfort to the enemy. Social movements would like to present a united front to the world at large. Like all human endeavors, though, they are full of people going off on their own tangents and tripping each other up.

"Reality," says Hazel Henderson, "is what you pay attention to." There is too much of it for any one of us to take it all in. We have to pick and choose. In the process of choosing, we bring to bear the special collection of values, biases, interests, and experiences that we embody (in lieu, I suppose, of ideal qualities). We may call this process reason, but in truth, reason forms only a part of it. Our "unreasons"—our feelings, intuitions, values, and biases—play a part that is just as important.

Eventually, each of us finds a special wavelength we can call home. This wavelength will differ from those others have chosen, and these differences will provoke all kinds of honest conflict among people otherwise in complete agreement about the vision or goal they share. What this means, of course, is that the vision is being examined a thousand different ways, the goal is being approached from an infinite number of directions. This is entirely desirable. If the vision is to be realized or the goal to be reached, then all possibilities must be explored, no routes must be closed off. We mustn't put all our eggs in the one basket of my perspective or of yours. But I make the mistake of thinking that my perspective is the only valid one and you mistakenly decide that yours is, and so we get into a fight.

There are many such things to fight over in social movements. To simplify, I have prepared this handy guide to the subtle conflicts that characterize all social change endeavors. It will not explain everything, but it will give you some idea of what is going on.

KENNARD'S ALL-PURPOSE LIST OF CONTRASTING, CONFLICTING PERSPECTIVES

Elitist	versus	Populist
National	versus	Grassroots
Global	versus	Backyard
Organization Builders	versus	Creative Anarchists
Professionals	versus	Volunteers
Board	versus	Staff
Staff	versus	Members

Paid	versus	Unpaid
Funded	versus	Unfunded
Experts	versus	Generalists
Reformers	versus	Radicals
Purists	versus	Pragmatists
Media-oriented	versus	Lobby-oriented
Up-front	versus	Behind-the-scenes
Insiders	versus	Outsiders
Old-timers	versus	Young Turks
Combative	versus	Facilitators
Exclusionsits	versus	Outreachers
Hierarchical	versus	Collective
Men	versus	Women
Solemn	versus	Irreverent

This list could go on forever, but you must have gotten the idea by now. What a mine field one must cross to render a bit of altruistic service to the dear old cause! Newcomers to the movement are especially endangered because they don't even know that the field is mined. They might be listening carefully to a debate and trying to understand the issues, learn the facts, and figure out the rules, when all of a sudden-bang!—something explodes. The newcomers are confused and hurt. For no apparent reason, a knock-down, drag-out fight has broken out and the newcomers find themselves in the middle of it. What happened, of course, was that somebody stepped on somebody else's toes.

It would be convenient, of course, if you could walk into the room and instantly detect everyone's special blend of motivations and perspectives, strengths and weaknesses. I suppose really good politicians can do this; I know that really good organizers can. Most of us, however, have to feel our way gingerly, one step at a time. But I <u>like</u> these little voyages of discovery. People come in all sorts of surprising combinations. To discover them, to learn just what makes them tick, is one of life's chief pleasures.

The myriad delights and contradictions that motivate human

beings are never more present or abundant than in social movements. An elitist expert might be working as an unpaid volunteer. A high-ranking male executive intensely focused on reform legislation in the Congress might also be a devout feminist. A housewife working in apparent isolation at her kitchen table might actually be the brains behind a powerful new cause. The genial, experienced old-timer, with thirty or forty years service, might actually be the most radical thinker around, despite what the Young Turks believe. An efficient organization builder, who ruthlessly promotes an institution, might turn out to be a superb nurturer of other people. And on and on.

So the next time some smart aleck attacks your movement on the grounds that its leaders aren't living the lives of the saints, let him have it. You don't have to bleed to death to prove to him or anyone else that you've made a commitment in good faith. The _cause_ is the thing that matters. You cannot embody the ideal because it's not humanly possible. Don't let anybody lay that trip on you. For that matter, don't lay it on yourself, either. Doing business on the side of the angels would be much easier if people in social movements would just lift their egos off this hook. And, for heaven's sake, don't _you_ lay this trip on somebody else.

Don't go seeking some perfect master whom you can worship or some peerless leader to whom you can give your heart. Sooner or later, he or she will only let you down when you discover that, alas, your leader is flawed after all. Besides, you're not doing this individual any favor when you dump a load of undiscriminating adoration on him or her. This may sound nice to some people, but really it is bad feedback to receive. With you rooting for him or her, the object of your affection might start believing in his or her own divinity. Soon this leader will decide he or she is infallible. When that happens, watch out. The infallible make lousy leaders. A truly able leader is ever conscious of his or her own fallibility and guards against it by constantly testing reality. Like Cromwell, this leader demands to see the warts painted in his or her portrait. But if you persuade somebody that he or she is without warts or other imperfections, your leader may act on that assumption and soon the whole shebang will come down around his or her head and yours too.

My advice is that you disenthrall yourself from the false image of peerless leadership and become your own leader. Find some decent people who share your commitments and with whom you can work. Believe me, that's the very best you can do. Yes, they will all possess a fault or two. But if you think about it, you will have to agree that you do too.

Stalking the Wild Idea

"First a new theory is attacked as absurd;" said Henry James, "then it is admitted to be true, but obvious and insignificant; finally it seems to be so important that its adversaries claim they discovered it." When my friend, the late E.F. Schumacher, author of Small Is Beautiful, first began expounding his ideas for alternative technology, the mandarins of science were quick to denounce him as a crank. Later when his ideas attracted a large following, these same mandarins would confront Schumacher at meetings and demand to know why he and his associates had produced so little alternative technolgoy, as if it were the easiest thing in the world to do! Now that Schumacher is conveniently dead and out of the way, some of these mandarins are traversing the globe delivering authoritative papers on the subject at international conferences. So the world turns, not only in science but in all things.

Social change always originates in disrepute. In some little neglected corner of society, a spark is struck and a new idea—wild, heretical, far out—occurs to somebody. Maybe this individual is an ordinary person who is wondering what to have for dinner as he walks down the street, or maybe he is some unrecognized genius who finally solves a puzzling problem he has been working on for years. In any case, the flash of insight occurs unbeknownst to the authorities. The political system, which we have been taught to think of as the principal vehicle for social change, is not informed that a powerful new idea is on the horizon until relatively late in the game. Although social movements ultimately address formal politics—the business of deciding who gets nominated and elected—they do so only after passing through a number of earlier stages.

Reading election returns is a poor way to detect impending social change. "None of the major changes in our society took place because of elections," writes author and columnist Garry Wills. "The elections ratify changes that have already taken place, legitimate those changes. . . . when we look for the forces of change (we find) that people who start out as 'freaks' generate change—Martin Luther King starting the bus boycotts, the teachers and students who began the first anti-war teach-ins on Vietnam, the first Suffragettes."

A lot of different people play a part in the initiation and advancement of social change, and there are many different parts to be played. Let's examine some of them.

The origin of social change usually results from the act or insight of an individual: an artist, a saint, a tinkerer, an angry housewife, a radical student. This person for some reason seizes the moment and the possibility it contains (such as Rosa Parks refusing one day in Birmingham, Alabama, to take a seat at the back of the bus). Whatever they do—write a book, burn a bra, get arrested, or chain themselves to a tree—such individuals get the social change ball rolling. They are the originators.

The act or idea of the originator strikes a responsive chord in a few people; something in them is ready for it. One by one, they step forward and begin to identify themselves to each other. Soon they form a network, an informal alliance of like-minded people willing to work voluntarily on behalf of some shared purpose or belief. These people—the networkers—go to work for the new cause of innovation with small hope of reward or recognition. No contracts or grants are to be had. No jobs or career opportunities await them in the field; indeed, no field as yet exists. But by raising issues not raised before, and by reconceptualizing old problems, networkers eventually provoke the emergence of new fields for public and private endeavor; but that comes later.

Gradually, people with grassroots political skills become interested in the new cause or innovation because it fits neatly into their own organizing agendas. For example, this was true of Schumacher's ideas. As an environmental organizer, I was busy promoting Small Is Beautiful because it justified environmentalism in economic terms. Imagine my surprise and delight when I learned that poverty and blue-collar organizers were equally enthusiastic about the book, not because it was proenvironment, but because it showed how millions of new jobs could be created. So grassroots organizers go to work forming committees, publishing newsletters, holding press conferences, staging fairs and teach-ins, holding rallies and marches.

While these expressions of grassroots ferment may be pervasive throughout the country, they are typically independent and uncoordinated. No central direction calls them into being. Perhaps informal information networks link them into a conscious whole, but that is about it. In essence, they are beyond the control of a centralized force and therefore uncoordinatable. They spring up naturally in response to the need for action. A good example is the citizens' movement against highways. At one point in the early seventies, there were 700 local antihighway groups around the country. Nobody in Washington, D. C., created them, unless you count the Federal Highway Administration whose road-building mania invited its own demise. Nobody gave these groups a grant or a contract. Nobody promised them jobs or promotions if they would take on the fight against highways. But there they were; 700 tiny, dedicated groups, many of which actually stopped roads from being built.

The spread of grassroots ferment soon begins attracting a new brand of followers: academics and professional people who want to help out by preparing the legal, scientific, and intellectual defenses of the cause. These are the public interest advocates and they spring up in Washington, D. C., and in the state capitals. Their job is to devise legitimacy for the new cause by proving that it works. They perform alternative research to demonstrate the technical feasibility and economic practicality of the new cause. They testify before legislative committees and public hearings; they prepare new legislation and see that it gets introduced; they bring law suits to bear. Skilled, professional lobbyists are hired and sent worming their way over Capitol Hill and through the executive agencies.

By this time, some politicians take up the cause. Of course, good politicians are always on the alert for new ideas that seem to have captured the public's fancy. To demonstrate just how good they are at leading, politicians will jump in front of whatever crowd is marching and proceed to lead it. This is a natural part of the social change process. After all, politicians (most of them, anyway) cannot afford to take the risks that social change advocates take. Politicians have to stand for reelection while conceptualizers, networkers, organizers, and public interest advocates do not. Quite reasonably, politicians shy away from a new cause in its initial stages of development. But once the new cause gains sufficient acceptance and backing, some politicians will fight the good fight on its behalf.

Eventually, new laws are passed and new public agencies are established to carry them out. Staff is hired, regulations are issued, contract and grant programs are set up. Naturally, academic institutions and consulting firms decide to go after the money. They recycle themselves in whatever direction the new agenda points. This tendency is all right, too; it represents just another beep on the monitor of social change. Academics and consultants will grind out massive, dull reports on the new priority until it eventually becomes conventional wisdom. So it goes. Finally, graduate students in the best schools in the land will begin writing dissertations on the history of the social movement that carried the cause to its eminent maturity. Usually, they get the story all wrong, but so what? The process of social change is indecipherable and so it should remain. We shouldn't, we can't eliminate the mystery. We don't want any dictators reducing the process to a science.

Perhaps this is why we so quickly erase from our memory the origins of social change. Being low-born, they are somewhat embarrassing to recall. The trade-off is clear and simple. We allow the formerly despised act to become enshrined while its perpetuators are dropped down the memory hole. For example, the Daughters of the American Revolution, not one of whom would lay a white glove upon the brutish arm of sacred authority, delight in celebrating the insurrection of their grubby forebears two centuries ago. All for the revolution, naught for the revolutionaries, unless they happened to be aristocrats like Washington or Jefferson.

So the citizen volunteers who painfully eased the new cause into the temple of respectability remain nameless and forgotten. Often, even the name of the originator is eliminated from the history. The process of social change is, in fact, so long, drawnout, diffused, and indirect that it is scarcely attributable to any one individual or group.

Naturally, some people demand a public association with the cause they embrace, which is highly egotistical. At whatever stage they come along in the process, these people need to feel that they are the prime movers behind the cause they endorse. This allows them to clothe their ego needs in the radiant garments of high moral purpose. Again, there is nothing wrong with this. Besides making people feel good about what they do, this identification unleashes the mighty force of individual self-expression on behalf of the cause-. Fighting for the cause-any cause-demands an almost superhuman investment of energy. Without such investment, the cause will soon dwindle and die.

Moral satisfaction is the true payoff for people who involve themselves in social change. It is quite a sufficient reward, much better in its own way than monuments carved of stone. Besides, once people who are primarily interested in their own deification get involved in a social movement, you can forget the poor dear old cause. Consider what happened when Stalin took over from the Bolshevik idealists. When the cause goes down the drain, it is sacrificed to the awful, ancient sin of pride. Given the choice, I would rather have social change continue to evolve in the same old humble way that denies recognition to its perpetuators, but grants them the quiet satisfaction of work well done.

Let the freaks of the world go on unveiling wild, new ideas, one of which out of a thousand will take its assigned place as the right idea at the right time. Let small groups of dedicated, self-selected adherents go on working voluntarily to spread the new idea and to build a political force on its behalf. Volunteer social movements offer their adherents an infinite range of choice: Creative anarchy springs up; diversity is the guiding principle.

Such social movements are hard at work in America right now, addressing such general concerns as air, water, land, food, shelter, health, jobs, energy, transportation, communications, consumer protection, and racial and sexual equality. At the moment, the citizens' energy movement is particularly visible. It started years ago, long before the government began to warn of the energy crisis, and it has devised a decentralized, many-pronged assault on the mammoth problem of energy. Citizen groups have formed around the issues of utility regulation, pricing, energy technology, conservation, safety, alternative uses, and scores of other things. The solar energy proponents comprise one of the more prominent movements under the general category of energy. Interestingly enough, this movement differs significantly from its sister phenomenon, the antinuclear movement. These two movements seem to appeal to basically different temperaments: The prosolar people are busy mounting the alternative energy scenario; the antinuclear people are busy unmasking the intrinsic, irreparable flaws of nuclear power. One movement builds, one attacks. Both are needed. Different people work at different tempos, employing different strategies and tactics. Yet they are entirely complementary and not in the least inconsistent. The prosolar people are generally antinuclear, and the antinuclear people are usually prosolar. They have chosen different paths. Diversity works!

All this diverse activity may appear to be random, formless, and inconsequential to the outside observer, but of course it is not. Small and humble as their origins are, social change movements ultimately weave a pattern so bold and clear that the image itself reorders an entire society. Knowing this, I can only plead that we be a little kinder in the future to citizen-based movements. Social change will never be an easy business; indeed, it should not be. The massive obstacles to change are there, I know, for a purpose. Only the best new ideas—those tested and tormented a thousand different ways—deserve to survive. These are the ones that grow stronger through their arduous passage and begin to flourish under adverse conditions.

Perhaps the obstacles to social change don't have to be as fierce and numerous as they now are, however. We are going to need many new social and technical innovations if we are to pick our way through the collapse of industrialism to the promise of the future. Maybe we ought to welcome the far-out; maybe we should invite heresy; maybe we ought to go stalking the wild idea. The woods are full of them.

When Nobody Was Looking, Our Side Won

Looking back over the past few decades, we can see that industrialism's adverse consequences made inevitable the rise of environmentalism, just as earlier they made inevitable the rise of organized labor. Industrial workers found themselves confronted by a cold, clear choice: Organize or be trod into dust. So they organized. Citizens observing the increasing pollution of the planet came up against the same kind of choice: Organize or be poisoned. And so they organized.

The human species is imbued with the life force. It balances our impulse toward self-destruction. We are not going to exit from the planet without putting up a good fight. Therefore, a certain inevitability attends the rise of social movements. If you hitch your wagon to such an inevitability, you are bound to go places.

As any citizen activist can tell you, pursuing the inevitable is dreadfully hard work. The hours are long, the pay is poor or nonexistent, and the amount of personal responsibility you must assume is enormous. But you do score occasionally. As an environmentalist, I was pleased to come across this statement by Llewellyn King, editor of the trade journal entitled <u>The Energy Daily</u>, and no special friend of the cause. "The fact is that the environmentalists have won, and it has to be said that their achievements in a few short years have been massive. What they have achieved is an institutionalization of concern for the environment at every level of national life. From now on a concern for the environment will be a fundamental part of civilized life. It is impossible to contemplate a society that will not weigh the impact of its actions upon the earth's ecology in the future. No social movement in this century has been so totally effective in so short a time."

The environmental movement won because, in a free society, <u>authentic social movements always win</u>. The real question is, what constitutes victory? It turns out that paradise on earth is not in the cards. Is the planet cleaner than it was before the environmentalists came along? Maybe a little in some places, but on the whole, probably not. Are ecosystems more stable and secure than they were ten years ago? Probably not. Has the human species been granted a new lease on life? Only time will tell. In some ways the peril to the planet continues to increase despite the efforts of environmentalists. For example, the use of toxic substances has increased dramatically in the past ten years with who knows what disastrous future consequences. This is victory?

Victory, like love, is where you find it. I think the environmentalists have aided society in averting some genuine catastrophes and in mounting some countertrends to industrialism's worst traits. Some of the most obvious forms of pollution have been brought under control and in some places air quality and water quality have improved somewhat. But this isn't where victory is found.

The real gains scored by the environmentalists have been intellectual, education, moral, and political. To me, environmentalism represents the most potent and profound critique of industrialism that has yet appeared. This critique is transforming industrialism for the better.

Environmentalism has also secured a great change in consciousness around the planet. In 1970 the very word ecology was hardly known. Today any schoolchild can tell you what it means. As citizen educators, the environmentalists have succeeded beyond their fondest hopes. This tastes of sweet victory to me.

Then too, many new legal, regulatory, and administrative processes have been set in motion by environmentalism; and while getting them adopted was exceedingly cumbersome, time-consuming, and exhausting work, these processes are slowly altering the climate in which public and corporate decisions are made. More and more often, the true social and economic costs of industrial expansion are being figured in public policy. More and more often, corporate executives are accepting environmental protection as a standard part of doing business. As a result, both public policy and corporate plans are becoming more morally responsible. These changes have also had the effect of buying time for social and technical innovations to take root and grow. Now, buying time may not satisfy those environmentalists in desperate psychological need of a clear, discernible event that can be hailed as a triumph, but they ought to relax a bit and feel secure in the knowledge that buying time is sometimes the best we can do. A lot of wars have been won because the ultimate victors knew when to play for time and let the glory go.

Resign yourself philosophically to the inevitability of change and you will find solace. It may not be as swift as you wish it to be or as complete, but it will come. The life experience of each of us provides abundant proof of this. When you encounter friends whom you have not seen for a few years, you may be amazed at how they have changed. Perhaps they dress or wear their hair differently. Perhaps they have aged or lost or gained weight. Perhaps they behave differently or hold new opinions. Perhaps in the intervening period their lives were touched by love or tragedy or religious experience. Fashions change, bodies change, minds change, spirits change. And so do social values. Look at the attitudes in America today and contrast them with those of the fifties. The fifties seem as remote from us as the Middle Ages and all the reactionary attempts to bring them back are doomed to fail.

Since the inevitability of change is so obvious, I always wonder why so few people consciously exploit this certainty. Why not learn to detect the character and direction of impending change? Why not welcome it and dance to its music?

It isn't all fun and games, of course. There are risks. Leaders of social change movements have been murdered, jailed, exiled, spied upon, mocked, scored, and otherwise persecuted. They are nearly always denounced as dangerous radicals or foolish crackpots. Not surprisingly, these risks keep a lot of people out of the social change business.

Another drawback is that recognition of the contributions made by innovators is often too little and too late. The "radical" program of young William Jennings Bryan was finally implemented by "progressive" Woodrow Wilson. It took twenty years for the ideas to gain legitimacy. Norman Thomas ran for president half a dozen times and his candidacy was derided, but liberal Democrats under Franklin D. Roosevelt ultimately appropriated much of Thomas's program without so much as a thank-you note.

The consolation prize for social innovators is that ultimately their agendas get adopted. Use, as I do, a broader time frame for looking at these things. From a higher vantage point, looking into the future, I believe one can say that the antinuclear movement has "won." The technology is not only unsafe, it is economically unsound, as Wall Street has now recognized. Again, the citizen analysis was better than that of industry or government. I believe too that the appropriate technology movement has won and that we are bound to see tremendous advances in small- and intermediate-scale technological alternatives. I believe that the movements for racial and sexual equality have won in the sense that they have so forcefully advocated the new values they embody and that these values are lasting. It is impossible to conceive of conditions under which racial minorities and women would return to their prior subservient status. Too many of them are willing to fight to the death to avoid it. Such intense commitment cannot be defeated by force. So long as the commitment remains, the new age is evolving. Don't look now, but I think we're winning.

Sorcery in the Public Interest

In 1970 I joined a small band of citizens determined to halt American manufacture of the supersonic transport. Although most of us were already deeply engaged in other, seemingly more consequential issues—Vietnam, nuclear power, the Highway Trust Fund—the SST appeared to be a worthy new target for several good reasons, both strategic and tactical.

Despite its extraordinary and apparently unassailable backing by big business, big labor, the Nixon administration, and key members of Congress, the SST was in fact increasingly vulnerable. Its technological design was under fire, especially on ecological grounds. The threat of damage to the upper atmosphere and the undeniable problem of sonic booms seemed grave enough, but there were economic questions too. The SST's great cost (largely to be borne by taxpayers) seemed unjustifiable alongside its slight contribution to transportation. Most of the people who would foot the bill for the SST would never in their lives have the opportunity or the money to fly it. Transporting a few affluent people higher and faster across the ocean didn't seem like much of a priority when compared with easing traffic congestion in American cities or a hundred other things.

In many ways, the SST seemed a symbol of the nation's outmoded, distorted priorities and of so much else that had gone wrong with the country: decision-making in a back room by a few powerful corporate and political leaders; boundless, idiotic faith in high technology as a remedy for social problems; and manipulation of citizens and consumers through spurious economic justifications and slam-bang public relations campaigns.

Besides the tactical opportunity to exploit the SST's negative symbolism, there also existed this beautiful advantage: The SST hadn't been built yet. Compare this tactical setting with, say, that of citizens fighting the highway/automobile industrial complex. Obviously, thousands of miles of highways have been built and millions of automobiles have been manufactured to traverse them. The industrial complex that produced all this obtained a stranglehold on the American economy in the process. Loosening this grasp is the goal of many civic action groups, but they are fighting impossible odds. Stopping the SST, on the other hand, was a way of nipping a technology in the bud before it grew so large that social processes could not contain it.

And then there was the sweet possibility of victory. A small, but visible, chance existed to withdraw American support for the SST. Every once in a while social movements need to experience something akin to victory. It's good for morale. It attracts new followers. It convinces the press and the politicians that the movement is real and later on this impression helps when the going gets rougher and no discernible victories are in view.

So we decided to take on the SST, knowing full well that, despite our tactical advantages, we were going up against the full weight of the business lobby, the labor lobby, and the administration. The aerospace industry determined to wage a holy war on behalf of the SST and made it a clear test of corporate power in America. They claimed that failure to produce an American SST would be to surrender our technological leadership and would make us a second-rate nation. They raised a lot of money for a pro-SST campaign and hired public relations firms to unleash a barrage of pro-SST propaganda. And there we stood armed with . . . . what?

We beat the American SST. It took a long time and much hard work. <u>How</u> we did it is a story that has never been adequately told, and it will not be adequately told here. The tale cannot be done justice. Like most important citizen victories, the battle against the SST was won through a humble, quiet, decentralized process of voluntary social collaboration called, if there is a name for it at all, citizen networking. In a network, countless people participate informally, doing what they can where they are, linked only by information and bonds of trust.

How many people fought the SST? I cannot tell you. Ten thousand? A million? I have no way of knowing and neither does anyone else. Networking is such a loose, ephemeral process that it is impossible to attack, thank goodness. What can be tracked can be hunted down and captured or killed. Networking is anarchistic. Without waiting to be told what to do, citizens simply go to work on their own, using the tools at hand to mount a political action or to build public understanding of some new idea or cause.

What did the people fighting the SST do? In this case (though not in all, by any means), lobbying the Congress was the name of the game. Specifically, our target was to withdraw further federal subsidies for the development of an American SST. To this end, three distinct kinds of networking evolved: a political network on Capitol Hill for information-gathering and lobbying purposes; an intellectual network of scientists and other academics critical of the SST and willing to speak out against it; and a grassroots network of local citizen activists all across the country, each of whom, by the way, possessed a network of his or her own reaching into every corner of the community. In this way we covered all the bases.

For my part, I was responsible for covering a number of states where my personal network was strong. In most principal cities of these states, I tried to maintain at least two or three key contacts. I had all their office and home telephone numbers. In order to launch action from any congressional district for which I was responsible, all I had to do was reach one of my contacts. Chances were that I could always reach one of them at any hour, day or night.

When President Nixon called a senator to the White House to persuade him to vote for the SST, we would soon know about it, sometimes within an hour. Though we never had more than two or three people working full-time on the anti-SST campaign, they were plugged into other public interest and environmental lobbyists on Capitol Hill who volunteered to keep eyes and ears peeled for us. They passed on every tidbit they picked up and so we were superbly informed. After I had been alerted, I would get on the phone. When the senator who had been pressured by the president walked into his office the next day, he would find an impressive pile of phone messages and telegrams from back home urging him to vote against the SST.

Meanwhile, the attack on the SST's intellectual justification continued unabated. Engineers, scientists, and economists volunteered their time and talent to work against the SST. If cost/benefit analysis was to be used to justify the project, then all right, we would use cost/benefit analysis to hoist it on its own petard. A stunning blow was dealt the SST when fifteen prominent economists, ranging from Milton Friedman on the right to John Kenneth Galbraith on the left, condemned the project on economic grounds.

The anti-SST forces in the Congress, led by Senator Proxmire and armed with a reputable counteranalysis of the SST, aided and abetted by public interest and environmental lobbies, and immeasurably strengthened by signs of widespread citizen revulsion against the project, finally secured a series of votes that rang down the curtain on the American SST. On the night after the last vote, we celebrated our victory as indeed we had every right to. In and of itself, halting the SST was a tremendous achievement. But that night we hardly dared speculate on what our victory really portended. Perhaps we didn't know it, or perhaps we thought it too audacious to say out loud, but that night the momentum of industrialism—the prevailing pattern for 200 years—was broken, at least symbolically and momentarily.

Because I think history will bear me out on this, I sometimes make the claim that the defeat of the SST signified a turning point in human affairs. For the first time, the values of industrialism had been rejected in a clear contest over values. For the first time, citizens revolted against a technology directly and in advance of its application, not just against its adverse consequences after the fact. It seems to be that the defeat of the SST eroded the mystique of technology and, without a romantic spell to gloss over its cruder and more violent character, technology has been judged more harshly ever since.

For a century or more, industrial complexes had been able to ram through virtually any technological scheme they wanted. For decades, Congress voted federal subsidies in abundance for practically any technological proposition that came along. It did so in the belief that technology was a cornucopia from which all good things—jobs, progress, growth-spouted endlessly. The rejection of the SST dramatically signaled the rise of public disenchantment with technology. A warning shot was fired across the bow of swift-sailing industrialism. Never again could industrialists operate in perfect complacency, sure of their ability to manipulate politics and government at will. Sure, they still exercise great power and they still get their way more often than not, but they have been put on notice. And, most importantly, the spell was broken. Without the mystique of technology, industrialists must rely on crude force to get their way. They are prepared to do that, but the battle lines are becoming clearer to everyone. We see more clearly what's at stake: our health, our neighborhoods, our futures. They will not always win.

No new giant technological scheme can be mounted today without someone demanding, and frequently obtaining, a rigorous examination of its full social, economic, and environmental impacts. No such project can be designed without its designers being aware there is a chance that society will reject it. This change, compared to the old days, is profound. It signifies the transformation of industrialism.

Social advances along these lines—that is, shifts in basic values—are to me more consequential than any electoral or legislative victory, although such victories often reflect a value change that has already occurred. The vote in Congress against the SST was an unusually strong and clear sign of shifting values. It resulted from an unusually strong and clear exercise in citizen networking, a process most people ignore or take for granted. But to me, networking is a social tool possessing almost magical qualities. How else could a handful of people (so it seemed) with no money, no conventional power or prestige, and no army of legal and technical mercenaries at their command take on corporate America and stand it on its ear? When the citizen networks took on the SST fight, corporate America didn't know what hit it. When assaulted in this manner, it is customary for corporate leaders and their political allies to foam at the mouth and rave about communist plots. Fortunately, I can ease their tortured minds on this score. What defeated the SST was not a communist plot, but an exercise in democratic citizenship so creative and anarchistic that it resembled sorcery.

Doing It with Mirrors

What is a citizen network? To begin, networks are not formal organizations. Hazel Henderson, futurist and social critic, describes them beautifully:

> They have no headquarters, no leaders, and no chains of command. They are free-form and self-organizing, composed of hundreds of autonomous, self-actualizing individuals who share a similar view and similar values. . . they are evanescent, ebbing and flowing around issues, ideas, and knowledge. Their chief product is information processing, pattern recognition, and societal learning. Luckily, networks are linked by the mimeograph machine, the postal system, and the telephone—all decentralized technologies accessible to individual users with constitutional guarantees of privacy. Networking cross-hatches all existing structured institutions and links diverse participants who are in metaphysical harmony. Networking is the most vital, intelligent, integrative organizational mode on our social scene. Perhaps this self-organizing mode represents a new maturing of human intelligence.

Since they are not prestigious institutions signifying permaence, authority, and dignity, citizen networks can afford to run risks, make mistakes, have fun, and create social innovations. Networking allows such freedom of expression and range of action that those who volunteer simply choose a spot on the line of battle where they wish to fight and dig in. Through a process we might call political alchemy, a common substance—local citizen action-is transmuted into the gold of constructive social change.

Because they are small and invisible, networks can look at things whole and obtain a clear picture of what is happening. The network's perspective is not obscured or distorted by institutional bias, political ambition, or monetary greed. Because career rewards do not come through networking, people are able to be honest in the give-and-take between them. They are not afraid they will lose their jobs if they tell the truth. Networks love truth, no matter how bad it is. Bad news is processed and transmitted as quickly and fully as good. Roll with the punches, look the facts straight in the eye, make the most of adversity: These are some of the rules of networking. There is no need of self-deception in networking. Here is one place where honesty is indeed the best policy.

When you want action out of a network, you don't have to beg or cajole anybody. Networkers are already motivated or they wouldn't be in the network. This high level of self-motivation precludes the need for any hierarchy of command. No boards or committees have to meet, no administrative orders have to be issued, no complicated legal contracts have to be agreed upon. Except for a telephone, no big expensive technologies have to be purchased. If I had to, I could run my network out of a telephone booth; I have run it many times out of a motel room.

This is why, when the time comes to act, networks can act with incredible speed. Networks go to work more directly and much faster than organizations can. Because so much time has already been spent clearing the channels, no static obscures the alert signal when networkers give it. The network channel is always clear. And because networkers are self-organizing, the messages transmitted through network channels don't have to include detailed instructions, as from a superior to a subordinate. All you have to do is press the alert button. The network will take care of the rest. The basis in shared values, the high level of trust, and the absence of rewards to fight over combine to give the network terrific logistical advantages.

Big established systems being quietly undermined by the force of networking seldom realize what is happening to them. They are too complacent and arrogant to think that some unorganized rabble could affect their power and prerogatives. Besides being sinful in and of itself, such pride is also a form of stupidity. This too plays into the hands of the networkers. To be counted beneath contempt is a wonderful tactical advantage. Your opponent, disdaining to acknowledge your existence, does not know where to hit back when you strike at him. Networks are so small, slight, and nimble that they are difficult targets to bring into focus.

Because they are beneath notice and even beneath contempt, citizen networks can instigate some measure of social change when no one is looking and then slip into the anonymous safety of mass culture. They do not stick around to claim credit for their work. If they did, they might get coopted or even bumped off. Interchangeable leaders and roles in the network also make it an impossible target. You might be a grand strategist one day and a common foot soldier the next. In the environmental movement, for example, I was a principal architect; in the antiwar movement, I made posters, circulated petitions, marched, and housed demonstrators.

Networks operate on almost no money. The biggest problem is how to pay the phone bill. But even the lack of funds has its advantages. Networkers soon learn not to waste a penny or a minute of time. Reliance on physical resources must be minimized and this necessity mothers invention. It is no accident that networkers become innovators. Another result is that networkers become splendid managers. They can do more with a dime than a bureaucrat can do with a thousand dollars. The absence of money has this added advantage: If you do not have a grant or a contract, your opponents cannot cut it off. Unencumbered by funding, the networker learns to devise tactics of daring simplicity. Organizations, with ever-constant money hang-ups, can never operate so ingeniously.

Networking is nothing new. It is as old as the hills. When hunting, Indians traveled in groups of twelve. They had learned that a group this size was large enough to function effectively and safely, but small enough to move quietly and quickly. The need is to obtain and pool the requisite data with no unnecessary complications. The early Christians must also have been superb networkers. How else could a small and despised sect linked by shared belief and bonds of trust spread their gospel to the far corners of the world in an astonishingly short time?

I find history full of marvelous networkers. My favorite is Talleyrand, the aristocratic French statesman and diplomat, whose conservative vision of peace and stability in Europe led him to serve and then to undermine half a dozen regimes. He helped bring down the Bourbon Monarchy, the Directory, Napoleon's empire and then, for good measure, the Bourbons again. Talleyrand lived in dangerous times. For protection, he assumed for himself the not uncongenial pose of someone lazy and frivolous. Talleyrand knew that serious, energetic men are easy marks for destruction. It so happened that most of Talleyrand's collaborators were brilliant, high-born women of the shrewd, witty type that dominated much of French history and culture. Whenever he was brewing a coup d'etat, the authorities always set spies in his household to see if they could catch him in the act and prove his treason. But the spies always reported back to their masters that Talleyrand couldn't be up to any mischief for all he did was play cards with the ladies! Talleyrand's blow, however, would always come and when it did it fell with deadly accuracy.

Networking and the Decentralist Ideal

Networkers sometimes look as if they are engaged in innocent or frivolous pursuits, but often they are weaving schemes of great consequence. Today, as industrialism wanes, anxiety stalks the land. Most people are convinced that life in the future is going to be markedly worse than it is now. This is not the first time that the human race has felt itself at the edge of a precipice and about to fall off. Nor will it be the first time that our ability to devise social and technical innovations will pull us back from the of destruction.

Lewis Mumford, writing in Technics and Civilization, describes the despair that pervaded civilization at the end of the Middle Ages: ". . . the old synthesis had broken down in thought and in social action . . . men lived in an empty world, a world that was daily growing emptier." But as the old order collapsed, a fresh one bloomed. Mumford observes that "it is just at the moment of cultural and social dissolution that the mind often works with a freedom and intensity that is not possible when the social pattern is stable and life as a whole is more satisfactory."

In the midst of cultural ferment, many new social and technical innovations are likely to emerge. Mumford describes how the printing press appeared at the close of the Middle Ages "to release people from the domination of the immediate and the local." Important social innovations—the university, the scientific academy, the industrial exhibition—also emerged in this era and the cumulative impact of these innovations ushered in the Renaissance.

If Mumford's reading of history is accurate, then maybe we ought to take some time off from hand-wringing and cursing each other and begin to look for signs of breakthrough, instead of breakdown. Many such signs exist if you know where to look for them. In America today, a countless number of barely perceptible citizen networks are hard at work producing social and technical innovations. They are addressing virtually every physical and social dimension of human communities. These networks are an organic response of the living to the self-destructive impulses of a waning value system. People are not about to let industrialism destory their culture or their environment. Not even the president of an electric utility would allow nuclear wastes to be buried in his backyard. Eventually, the entire population of our planet will get into the act, rebelling against the costly, unreliable, dangerous, and job-destroying technologies being shoved down its throat.

People fighting nuclear power plants in their area find they have much in common with people waging similar fights in Australia, Japan, France, or Denmark. Thus, the antinuclear movement has become a worldwide phenomenon, as has its sister movement, the prosolar phenomenon. Social movements ultimately become international in scope as networks extend their sway over the globe. Tiny "radical" parties dedicated to ecology, feminism, cultural diversity, and alternative technologies have sprung up in most parts of the world and, though they have garnered few votes so far, their influence upon the future of politics may be extraordinary.

What is the program being advanced by citizen networks? Does it add up to any coherent whole? The networks place a common stress upon the preservation and revival of <u>diversity</u> in every form: animal, biological, cultural, racial, sexual, technological, and aesthetic. Networks value diversity for its own sake, seeing it as a sort of insurance policy for the human race, a force for balance and stability within the social system. Accordingly, a consistent theme found in most networking is the search for <u>alternative solutions</u> at alternative political and geographic scales. Among networkers, conventional wisdom is never to be blindly obeyed, but automatically suspected. Isn't there another, better way to do what needs to be done than the old way?

The search for alternatives is complemented and reinforced by the theme of <u>decentralism</u> found in much networking. Since networks are themselves perfect manifestations of decentralism, they have a keen and tested appreciation of the benefits decentralism brings. Making things smaller makes them easier to comprehend and to manage; it restores the possibility of personal accountability for the acts of individuals within the social system.

In contrast to the public apathy and dependence that industrialism appears to induce, the networks have renewed insistence for public participation in government and democratic control of social institutions. The idea of local self-reliance through local control of political and economic institutions is matched by the idea of personal self-reliance, achieved through simpler lifestyles, reduced consumption, meaningful work, and care for each other instead of depending on big institutions to do it. Thus, networks seek a new synthesis, a sense of the whole, which allows the individual and the community to strike a better balance between their diverse, conflicting needs.

It is important to remember that these trends have not been summoned into being by centralized authority. They sprang up on their own, or appeared to, through the medium of networking. True, once trends gain a certain momentum, a second stage of growth occurs wherein actual organizations, usually citizen-based and volunatry, enter the picture. But organizations are not networks and networks are not organizations. This important distinction is frequently misunderstood or ignored. I have even seen ads in magazines urging readers to "join a network" by paying a membership fee to some organization. To the true networker, this causes pain.

Let's examine the differences between networking and organizational stages of development. Networks are good at discerning and introducing brand new things or ideas. Organizations represent the initial social acceptance of the network's initiative. Once a network builds understanding of the new, the organization works to form this understanding into a publicly discernible political constituency. Organizations assert the new thing or idea in more obvious, conventional ways than networks do. They get a law passed on its behalf or they publish a journal about it.

Networks tend to be decentralist in perspective; organizations tend to be centralist in their view, that is, they focus on the functions of centralized organizations. Networks arise at the point where new problems or possibilities first occur, that is, at the local or regional scale. Only later is the matter perceived to be a national problem or possibility requiring national action. Due to understandable differences in these two perspectives, networks tend to be more covert and radical while organizations tend to be more overt and reformist.

Networks are informal; they aren't even incorporated. Usually, organizations are legal entities. Networks are nearly always unfunded. Networkers pay the costs of their own participation and occasionally the hat is passed to pay for essential, minimal costs. Organizations are funded by membership dues, foundation grants, gifts from wealthy individuals, and sometimes by government contracts.

Networks have no paid staffs so no seed of bureaucracy lies within them. They are formed and facilitated by unpaid generalists, usually by women. Organizations have paid staffs. They are led by trained, experienced administrators or by specialists such as lawyers or scientists. Networkers tend to be generalists; organization leaders tend to be analysts. Accordingly, networks tend to argue on moral and ethical grounds, while organizations argue on legal, scientific, or economic grounds.

Networks originate social change and clear the way for its advancement. Organizations facilitate social change and serve the needs of the new social change constituency once it has arisen. The remoteness of networking from money and conventional power enables it to perform very special functions. If money or conventional power is introduced into networking, it poisons the wells of trust and free cooperation on which networking depends. Organizations, because they address "real" things, run the risk of becoming bogged down or even contaminated. Real power is a nasty business; it brings out the worst in people. The closer you get to it, the nastier it becomes. Still, real things do happen to be real.

Gold and silver are real, just as bombs and toxic wastes are. Since they create all kinds of problems for us, somebody has got to address these real things for they will not go away on their own.

In order to operate, all that networks need is high-quality information transmitted through channels of trust. Participants in the network have a right to expect that data transmitted through the system is clear, reliable, timely, and confidential. Because networking is intensely personal—it consists mostly of direct, one-on-one interaction, usually over the telephone—subtle, refined, and sensitive information can be securely transmitted through it. This intimate, faithful level of exchange builds over time and constantly improves itself. Bad players, if they somehow slip into the game, are shown the door before they can figure out what is going on. For example, if I pass A to B in my network, B provides A complete access to B's data. In effect, I have certified to B that A is reliable and trustworthy. Should A prove not to be so, that is usually detected quickly and the network closes its doors to A the next time he comes around. Or, should B later find occasion to go to A for data and finds A unwilling to share it, B informs me of this transgression and I am expected to take corrective action. I am held responsible, as well I should be, for anyone whom I introduce into the network.

Networks operate on a high measure of reciprocity; in this, they are very businesslike. Participants are not only expected to be reliable and trustworthy, they are expected to put in as much as or more than they take out. Each one is expected to possess a well-organized, up-to-date data base inside his or her head. Each is expected to contribute analysis as well as raw data. Each is expected to share generously and honestly, for among the many webs that link the network is one of shared obligation to each other. I owe you, you owe me. If I hold back on you or you on me, the end of networking is near and neither one of us really wants that to happen.

Because networking is a communication-based activity cemented by trust and shared commitment, it is difficult to predict or forestall. There are few memos to intercept and no phones worth tapping, because there is no chain of command or orders passed down the line. Indeed, there is no line because networks are not linear as are the structured worlds of corporations and government bureaucracy. Even public interest groups have lines of command to contend with and, being democratic in character (or at least in intent), they can get bollixed up on these channels even worse than government agencies. Networks, being utterly democratic in character, and having no hierarchy to deal with, don't have to worry about paying lip service to group process or standards of accountability; they embody them.

Reduce the Membership and Strengthen the Party

Whether they know it or not, nearly everyone engaged in advocating social change is probably networking in some form or another. Networking is so humble and basic a process that you can fall into it almost without knowing it. It feels good, so you continue. It seems to work, so you continue further. Soon you are a full-fledged networker operating out of sight, but right beneath the nose of sacred authority. Yes, it's a trick, but one most networkers soon learn.

Indeed, some of the best networkers I know did not consciously realize they were networking until somebody tapped them on the shoulder and told them that's what they were doing. They simply weren't aware that they had stumbled upon a special process of social collaboration. They were just doing the work they had to do in the best way they knew how, guided by intuition, ingenuity, and direct, personal experience.

I think the best networks are personal and faithfully reflect the personalities of the networkers themselves. However, a network is not the same as one's groups of friends. I have dear friends, for example, whom I have known for years and who don't have a clue about my networking. We relate to each other on entirely different grounds. Maybe we used to be neighbors or we worked together in the same office years ago. Or maybe we like the same kind of music or theater, but networking doesn't enter into our relationship at all.

On the other hand, there are people in my network with whom I have no social relationship at all. Networking alone constitutes the basis of our interaction. Apart from that, we might never in a million years find a basis for a purely social relationship. I have some wonderful collaborators in my network whom I have never laid eyes on. We have done business for years over the telephone—satisfying, effective business, to be sure—but business all the same. Still, when it comes to pass, as it sometimes does, that I get the chance to meet these people in the flesh, it is always a great joy.

Some people are born networkers, some become networkers, and some have networking thrust upon them. Some people seem born—simultaneously blessed and cursed—with a sense of responsibility for the community as a whole. These dearly beloved, inveterate do-gooders form the rock upon which much desirable social change rests. Whether they represent the accidents of fate or a particularly lucky toss of the genetic dice, they are to be cherished. They often take to networking like a duck takes to water.

Some people become networkers in the course of doing something else: working in a political campaign, organizing a civic event, or seeking a new interest outside of homemaking, a motivation that leads many women into volunteer work. These people sometimes find that conventional do-gooding—the "nice" stuff—gets to be a bore. They learn that the real problem is corruption at city hall, and off they go to combat it. If they persevere at this much tougher duty, they may wind up networking.

Then there are those who are led to networking almost against their will. Suppose you learn that your home is about to be taken away from you, your apartment building is going to be converted into a condominium or a hotel, your house lies in the path of a proposed freeway, or that a fast-food restaurant is to be built directly across the street. You can surrender and move, or you can pick up your telephone and organize your neighbors to fight back. It may be years before you win and you may not win at all, but in the meantime, there is a good chance you will become a networker.

What size are networks? As I said, I think the best networks are personal ones, that is, no bigger than the number of people you can manage to relate to effectively on a personal basis. What size is this? There's no easy answer. It's clear to me at least that big is bad. I follow the rule laid down by Lenin: Reduce the membership and strengthen the party! But networking is a two-way street. I have a network, you are in it. You have a network, I am in it. Every networker possesses a sizable, but invisible, constituency. When I communicate with my network, I am communicating with a great many people, at least potentially. After twelve years of organizing, I can count about 500 people in my network. If every person in my network possesses a constituency of 100 people (a modest guess), then I might be addressing 50,000 people if I activate the whole thing. And these are 50,000 politically savvy, energetic, active citizens. Not many politicians can command such a force, nor many organizations, either. But then, networks cannot be commanded. Therein lies the difference.

Why do people network? In this day and age, networks offer people a rare chance for satisfying, communal action. This is their real magic. Networkers become sorcerers in the public interest simply by unhooking their egos from the conventional reward system. We refuse to behave like Pavlov's dogs. Networking is a healthy, constructive way to serve self <u>and</u> community while avoiding ugly clashes of power and greedy fights for glory. Networks offer people a form and source of psychological affirmation that is desperately needed today. I could never find love in a mailing list, but I can find it in a network. When I get blue, I get on the telephone and network for two or three hours. I may hang up exhausted, but I hang up happy.

People who are both sensitive and responsible don't have to look very far in the world today to become either despondent or outraged. Fighting back seems so futile that it seems easier to have another beer and forget about it. Networking overcomes this sense of powerlessness. Working unconventionally, you <u>can</u> change things for the better. Although some readers will have to forgive me for saying so, networking is a source of moral satisfaction. It feels good to do good, no matter how unfashionable such sentiments have become in this demoralized age. It isn't that one is enabled to adopt a smug, holier-than-thou attitude of the sort that has given morality a bad name. It's that one can achieve a quiet, inner satisfaction that needs no bragging about.

Networking is also a good way to obtain an education. When I joined the fight against freeways in the late sixties, nobody told me that along the way I would be forced to learn a lot about economics, law, science, and a dozen other fields. If I had been told, I would have turned and run in the other direction as fast as my legs could carry me. I didn't know I had the capacity to absorb all this knowledge and information. Besides, like most other kids in school, I had vigorously resisted even a nodding acquaintance with such dry, boring disciplines. But to fight freeways, I did learn them. I learned them in the context of bloody, applicable reality and I loved it.

Networking also teaches you political skills. You learn how to speak in public, how to organize committees, how to influence elections and legislatures, and how to use the media. In the process, you can have a lot of fun. Imagine, all this is for free and there are no stiff entrance requirements.

What is the future of networking? Some would say it is not all rosy. One apparent difficulty is that some business groups have caught on to the power of networking have begun to ape its tactics. For example, the loss of the bill to create a consumer protection agency was attributed to the aggressive grassroots lobbying of business groups. Every grocery store manager and shoestore owner in America got into the act at the behest of the U. S. Chamber of Commerce. How do I respond to this? I think, first of all, that any social tool ought to be available to everyone. Networking is an unusually potent tool and if business groups wish to employ it, they are within their rights to do so. But I don't think they will ever use it to maximum advantage for their motivation in using it—economic self-interest—will block them from fully understanding it. True networking is so intrinsically democratic, decentralized, and unconventional that I don't think business groups can go with the anarchistic flow of it. All the images in their heads are wrong for it. They see ordered structure as essential to any kind of collaboration; they can't comprehend creative anarchy.

Further, I persist in thinking that our form of politics still assigns a higher value to selfless action than to selfish action. Politicians may have to bow to the latter's fierce pressure, but most astute politicians actually welcome authentic grassroots pressure if only because it increases their own leverage and flexibility, and therefore power to decide. Moreover, I remain convinced that the moral authority emanating from well-organized, economically non-self-interested citizens will often outweigh the influence of the self-interested. I grant you my assumption that citizens will or can be well organized is a big one, but if you grant me that assumption, then I will stick to my argument that "right makes might."

But what about the use of networking by other citizen-based forces than those you or I happen to agree with? The anti-abortionists, for example, are not operating out of economic self-interest as business groups are. They are asserting an ethic, one that conflicts with another. What about their use of networking? All I can do is to repeat my belief that social tools are there for anyone to use. Because I have made up my mind on one side of the abortion issue doesn't mean that the debate is closed. Clearly, the debate is raging and it is a legitimate debate. If the anti-abortionists are out-networking the pro-choice people, then the pro-choice people will just have to work harder to persuade undecided or confused people of the rightness of their ethical position.

My own view of networking's future is unabashedly rosy. I don't see how it can fail. Being exposed constantly to the benign and nurturing influence of citizen networks has kept not only my sanity intact but my optimism as well. All the current talk about the "Me Decade" and the rise of narcissism falls on unreceptive ears when it reaches me. I think this interpretation of our time must come from urban, academic intellectuals who have never organized a bake sale or otherwise tapped into all the vitality and ferment at the grassroots. True, people may be turned off by the convulsions of politics and power—they are ceasing to vote in record numbers—but this doesn't mean that they are all sitting at home blissed out in a hot tub. To me, this means the true action may be elsewhere, in food cooperatives, in neighborhood organizations, or in citizen networks devising regional solutions to regional problems while ignoring artifical political boundaries. Such activities go undetected by social scientists because their rovings are so limited. Oh, well, they'll catch up in ten or twenty years.

The portents for networking are good because we have just begun to tap its potential. What I propose is that we use this fabulous tool more consciously and deliberately. What we did—innocently, and without plan—in the fight against the SST could well be done through rational design. If you have a difficult, innovative project to get off the ground—let's say the development of model solar villages—you might consciously build a system of voluntary support networks for it. One might consist of the intended consumer/inhabitants of the solar village; this support network, obviously, would exist on or near the site of the project. If the people to be benefited directly by the project are involved in it from the beginning, and if they are convinced in their own minds that the benefits are real, then they will work for it. Naturally, you will have to overcome initial distrust and suspicion from people who have learned to fear would-be benefactors, but if you employ the rules of good networking—patience, hard work, good faith, full disclosure, and other standard virtues—you will, with time, win them over. But in the course of this networking, you may learn that your solar villages need redesigning from the ground up. Your interaction with the people who will live there will teach you plenty if you are wise and humble enough to learn from them. One result, however, would make the entire effort worthwhile: The solar village would be much better designed when you were through.

Because your solar village concept is innovative and unusual, it might attract the interest and support of other change-oriented design professionals around the country: architects, planners, engineers and so on. Why not reach out and systematically build them into a support network for your project? The job of this network would be to provide a stream of intellectual defense for the solar village. You could probably tap the faculties of the best universities in the country for this purpose and, so long as you communicated with them faithfully, these allies in the professions might be willing to provide free consultation and criticism.

You might also build a political support network among sympathizers in Washington, D. C., both on Capitol Hill and in the executive branch, or in your state capital. Consult your network to identify possible supporters among legislators and public administrators and seek them out.

All this network support would be provided for free and on the quiet. It would be achieved informally through personal contact by trusted sources. No money would change hands. Only those people convinced or likely to be convinced of the project's social value would be approached. Nobody would be hit cold; they would be brought into the endeavor by personal contact and word of mouth. Remember that nothing sells like word of mouth. Eventually, when the moment is right, the stage set, and the lighting artistically arranged, you would go public with your concept with the networks singing its praises.

To non-networkers this scheme may sound improbable and may be inconsequential, but I swear to you on my address book that this just might work when nothing else will. Basically, most people want to be good and to help good things happen, but a lot of things get in the way: ego, competition, desire for reward and recognition, and a host of antihuman organizational motives and institutional imperatives. But the possibilities for constructive social change are still present and nothing on earth can eradicate them so long as human potential remains undiminished. Networking enables these lovely possibilities to stick out their heads, to test the air, and begin to breathe new life and hope into what sometimes seem utterly hopeless human predicaments.

Celebrations: How to Succeed in Politics without Really Trying

If you are absolutely certain you have turned up the right idea at the right time, and you wish to promote your discovery, why not give a party and invite the entire nation? I know you have few collaborators, no political power to speak of, and practically no money to spend, but don't let that stop you. Go out and organize a celebration!

I have been part of two mass national celebrations, Earth Day in 1970 and Sun Day in 1978, and I have seen how powerful such events can be. They work like magic, tapping human creativity and unleashing the energy it takes to launch new social movements. They provide a sense of constructive achievement: They can transform politics and our vision of the future. And they are even a lot of fun. Earth Day and Sun Day, I like to think, will ultimately have more real, positive impact upon society than a couple of national political conventions. Certainly, they provided a truer reading of society's present status and real options for the future than any party platforms have done. In retrospect, I believe both celebrations will be judged turning points of some consequence in history. If this is power tripping, what a way to go!

The ecological ideas promulgated by Earth Day are now actively transforming industrial societies into something better, and the solar age proclaimed by Sun Day opened up a hopeful new vista on the future. Earth Day sounded the trumpet; eight years later, Sun Day unveiled a well-conceived and practical technological and economic program for transition to the new age.

Both events received extraordinary coverage from the mass media. I think that no industrial corporation in America could begin to buy the amount of coverage that these events got for free. Through the communications media, millions of people all over the globe got the word that something new was afloat. To this day, when I meet environmentalists from other countries they press upon me their conviction that Earth Day here in America gave them their initial impetus too. It was a ploy heard round the world.

Politicians love celebrations. They don't want to be left out and they clamor to get aboard. On Earth Day in 1970, the Congress actually adjourned for the day so members could fly home to publicly swear their allegience to the cause of ecology. Seven months after Earth Day, President Richard M. Nixon, not exactly your typical ecology freak, established the U. S. Enviornmental Protection Agency. On Sun Day in 1978, President Carter traveled across the continent to take part in the celebration and shortly afterward greatly increased his administration's support for solar energy development. When I recall that both these events had been conceived only a few months before they took place by a handful of individuals, I am still amazed at the alacrity of the political response. For three or four years after Earth Day, environmentalists got virtually everything they wanted out of the Congress. And Sun Day put to rest for all time the till-then prevalent notion that solar energy was a nice idea but impractical for at least fifty years. In short, celebrations are a great way to play politics.

So what are you waiting for? Oh, you want to know just *how* to start. This gets a little more complicated. The hardest trick, as I have said, is to be sure you are riding the right idea at the right time. Without it, nobody will come to your celebration, whether you're planning a local or a global event. You will have to take your chances and I wish you loads of luck, because if your idea happens to be wrong—or even if it happens to be the right idea but at the wrong time—you will fall flat on your face.

But let's assume that you are indeed in possession of the right idea at the right time. Now you've got it made. All you have to do is unfurl a banner bearing the new insignia, and support will collect around you while the press beats a path to your door.

A vast amount of volunteer talent and energy will turn up

and go to work on behalf of your idea. Needless to say, this is a good thing, for celebrations must be produced for little money. They must be done on the quick and on the cheap. The entire budget for Sun Day, for example, was less than the cost of the solar exhibit the U. S. Department of Housing and Urban Development constructed in its lobby for the event!

Celebrations provide some valuable strategic and tactical advantages to the organizer. Usually, they are constructive in nature; they avoid or finesse ugly confrontations between competing power blocs. Sure, every organizer knows that confrontations are sometimes necessary and even desirable techniques. But celebrations are different. Instead of assaulting your congressman for his strong dam-building proclivities, you invite him to speak at an interfaith service in your town's largest church held to commemorate God's abundant natural diversity. A special prayer might be offered up on behalf of the snail darter. See what I mean?

Even community organizers tire of confrontation tactics. It's a nice change to adopt a positive tactic, especially if it has a hidden wallop. After all, there are really only two basic organizing techniques: the carrot and the stick. Community organizers certainly know how to wield the stick; we are much less skilled at waving the carrot. Celebrations are a good way to dangle a carrot in front of balky social institutions. Once in a while, they'll bite. Remember, it was a Republican administration that established the U. S. Environmental Protection Agency.

Celebrations say, in effect, we are (most of us, anyway) in agreement on certain basic values, and it's at least possible to envision working hand in hand to pursue them. This provides welcome relief from the dreary, endless clash of power blocs we call politics. True, your opponents include a lot of people you wouldn't trust any farther than you could throw them, but some of them, in their heart of hearts, really think of themselves as good guys. So stage a celebration and provide a nonconfrontational, noncontroversial context in which they can appear and swear upon a stack of Bibles that, yes, they do care for the preservation of life on earth, equal rights for women, black teenage employment, or whatever it is you are advocating. You will not win their souls, but the next time you have to come back to them to negotiate something, you will enter on a different wavelength. "If at first you don't succeed, try, try again."

In planning Sun Day, some people expressed the fear that high-technology companies would use the event to promote complex, large-scale, technologies (e.g., space platforms) that many advocates of decentralized technology oppose. Finally, we decided what the hell? We had no power to keep them out. Besides, if they came in we would challenge them to a debate on the merits of high- versus low-technology while the media looked on. We may have been a small group of citizens but we had the media's attention and the backing of a mass constituency. As it turned out, we were able to debate our differences.

Remember that celebrations are not mechanisms for resolving specific policy disputes. Celebrations embrace broad new goals. They do not adopt specific policy goals and they should not. Later, of course, you will have to zero in on narrow policy objectives, but this is not your purpose at the celebratory stage. (If you attempt this now, you may find yourself locked in struggle with even your friends and collaborators; people have a way of falling out with each other when it gets down to brass tacks.) The purpose of celebrations is to change the rhetoric, and to float new images before the eyes of people clouded or confused by the old. Celebrations alter the context in which future policy disputes are resolved. So the trick is to get everybody playing on new turf, a turf conceived and designed by you. Sun Day, for example, moved solar energy from its status as a relatively exotic technical option to the position of a broad social goal.

One word of warning: Celebrations require a light touch and a sense of fun. In no way does this detract from the seriousness of their purpose. The danger is quite the other way around. Some people attracted to social movements are deadly serious about their purpose, almost literally so.

The sincerity of such people is usually unquestionable and they are certainly useful when you're in a fight with a powerful, ruthless opponent. But these overly serious people are not temperamentally attuned to celebrations. They tend to be judgmental and intolerant of others. They are not prepared to joke about their goals or to make fun of themselves, to dance and sing in the streets and take part in the other giddy things that make up a celebration. When it comes to celebrations, they will blow it every time. So if it's possible to do so, leave the embittered ideologues at home while you stage your celebration. You will be glad you did.

While celebrations appear to take flight easily, the reality is that much work on their behalf has been completed in advance. The roots of Earth Day actually go back to the 1950s when small bands of citizens, usually the League of Women Voters, began to organize against water pollution. This same process originated the fight for clean air in the early 1960s when committees concerned about the ill effects of air pollution were formed in New York City and Los Angeles. By the time the student rebellion came along in the late sixties, the environmental cause had been carefully nurtured and networked to maturity. The time to unveil it on the world's stage had come. And so it happened. A lot of work must go on offstage so that magic can occur on it.

When all the chemistry is right, the social explosion occurs. Look at how these celebrations occur. They are gorgeous displays of creative anarchy. They are utterly decentralized, free-form, do-it-yourself phenomena. Yes, in some grubby little office in Washington, D. C., or New York City, banks of telephones are ringing off the hooks and sacks of mail are piling up full of requests for information on how to get involved. A small staff of underpaid coordinators struggles heroically with this deluge, but they are not "in charge" of it. They, along with everyone else who gets involved, are the lucky agents of the right idea at the right time.

Finally, I offer this observation on the almost mystical appeal of social celebrations. It has been said that is is always easier to revive something than to reform something. Celebrations work so well because they are revivals of human possibilities for a better life for us all. We <u>can</u> get our act together, and when we do, it's a hard act to follow.

Participation Makes Strange Bedfellows

Since the real decision-making power in government has shifted from politics (who gets elected) and even from legislation (what laws are passed) to technical administration, a new citizen movement has erupted upon the scene demanding more participation in the processes of administration. To me, this is perfectly natural and desirable. Citizens have gone, have been forced to go, where the action is.

Public administrators, with rare exceptions, view citizen participation in government processes with fear and loathing. They see it as a waste of time and money, a source of confusion, and the cause of ulcers. Public participation seems to them a peculiarly grubby form of politics, remote from and irrelevant to the intellectual and scientific quality of their work. After all, administrators may be compelled to cater to Congress, the press, and big business lobbies, but why should they have to interact with ordinary people who contribute nothing to the work they do?

Administrators are wrong to hold this view, I think, but I am not about to invoke the Constitution or even common courtesy to justify public participation in government. Instead, I wish to appeal to the self-interests of public administrators. I accept their self-interests as perfectly natural. They would not be human if they did not put their self-interests first. So let us skirt mere ethics here and get down to brass tacks.

For the purpose of this discussion, I am going to assume that public administrators want to do a good job of serving the public interest. I know that some people will jump on me for this, but I believe that not all public administrators in the land are corrupt or dishonest, stupid or incompetent. Clearly, some are but many aren't. Those administrators who are desirous of fulfilling their responsibilities under law are the people I have in mind. Why should they shoulder the admittedly heavy burden of public participation when there are so many ways to evade it?

As I see it, citizen participation and effective public administration go hand in hand. Properly performed, both tend to clarify and reduce the technical complexity in which most government programs are mired. Citizens ask the same basic questions that administrators must ask if they are doing their jobs right. For example, citizen groups concerned with environmental pollution ask these questions: How much pollution is there? Where does it come from? How does it affect us? What is being done about the problems it causes? Is the situation getting better or worse? If worse, why?

To administer a program, administrators must also employ such basic, clear questions. In a sense, administrators should ask such questions of their subordinates the first thing every morning. To have any chance of getting straight answers, it certainly helps to have people on the outside persistently asking the same questions. If we lose sight of the basic questions, we will all sink in the quagmire of technocracy, administrators included.

Aggressive citizen action and vigorous administration combined can make a balky system respond. Pressure must be consciously orchestrated from the top and the bottom, from inside and out, to make things happen. Administrators, after all, must be wary or they will soon fall under the sway of their subordinates, or of vested interests, or of collusions between the two. To protect and exercise power and initiative, they need room to maneuver. Citizen groups can help provide this flexibility by entering the fray from another direction. They serve as a countervailing force against both the technocrats and the vested interests. This can help the administrators buy time to work their own wills. Otherwise, they run the risk of winding up as puppets.

Government by special interests, as we all know, has grown into a real threat to our democracy. One result of this is the diminished power exercised by administrators. With all the talk of the wicked influence of special interests, some people—administrators among them—have made the mistake of lumping citizen organizations in the same category as corporate lobbies, professional associations, and labor unions. The environmentalists, for example, are routinely referred to as a "special interest group." This misses an important point. Whatever you think of them, it is hard to portray environmentalists as economically self-interested in the outcome of the issues they address. You can occasionally accuse them of elitism, insensitivity to social issues, bad science, or a thousand other things, but you cannot accuse them of being involved for the money.

Now it is perfectly legitimate to organize politically to defend one's economic interests. (Yes, even though money is the root of all evil.) But this is a far different thing, I submit, from organizing politically to defend the general interest. This distinction is important to administrators not because I expect them to grant special favors to altruistic motivation, but because they can exploit this fundamental difference to their own advantage.

How does this play into the hands of administrators? Information is power, right? Especially in a technocratic society. Now citizen groups are examining administrative activities and processes from a different angle. They are unpaid monitors of agency programs. Their analyses are rooted in different assumptions from either those of technocracy or vested interests. The information thereby generated is of great value to astute administrators. They can use it to avoid being hamstrung by people on one side of the debate. Often, the intelligence that citizen groups collect on agency activities contains information that would never otherewise reach the administrator. In every large agency, there is a sort of conspiracy on the part of the technocrats to keep the administrator overworked and exhausted, but underinformed and remote from the key processes and decisions. (This is only natural; the technocrats are working hard to maximize their discretionary authority too. It's just that I feel this is a game that the administrator, by rights, ought to win, if only because the standard of accountability the administrator must meet is higher than that of the technocrats.)

Citizen pressure can help rescue administrators from the

corner into which their subordinates and the vested interests are trying to paint them. What is a statesman, it is said, but a politician standing upright due to equal pressure from all sides? Administrators are in precisely the same spot. If they want to exercise power, they need citizen pressure to keep from collapsing under the weight of pressure from one side.

Let's look, for example, at a pollution control administrator. The pressure against effective control is obviously strong. It must be countered by equally strong pressure for effective control. Since the pressure against control comes from vested economic interests, which are well organized, and the pressure for control comes from the citizenry, which is less well organized, it makes sense for the administrator to actively solicit citizen involvement. This insures fuller and far more balanced representation of all affected interests. An administrator ought to openly solicit this involvement because it is intellectually honest and scientific to do so. The record should be as complete as possible before any decision is made. It is entirely defensible to seek out participation by absent or underrepresented interests to ensure a sound decision.

Often, the best way to obtain full participation is to facilitate the participation of voluntary civic organizations. They frequently possess splendid systems for alerting and educating their members. They deliver complex information far better than does any television news programs. After all, millions of people fork over their money to volunteer organizations for the purpose of receiving just such information. Moreover, citizen organizations operate within a context of mutual commitment to certain values. Those disseminating the information and those receiving it are linked by closer bonds than, say, the editors of a newspaper and its subscribers. Among many other functions, these bonds allow for a higher quality of interaction than mass media achieves. Again, from the self-interested perspective of the administrator, the quality of this alternative form of communication can become an advantage. It becomes a tool for getting out information to highly motivated people who are likely to turn out to participate in agency processes.

Since broad and diverse participation has the effect of increasing the options open to administrators, and thereby their flexibility and power, they should be prepared to put up with its drawbacks. Yes, public participation is a time-consuming process. But it is a good use of time. Just as it takes fine wine years to mature, it takes a long time to hammer out good public policy. And the process, when completed, delivers policies that stand a chance of actually working in the cold, hard reality of the world. Through public participation processes, the outcome has been pretested in the rough-and-tumble of social complexity. These processes provide the administrator with models of reality far more valid than those of any computer for they admit more variables. For example, the processes might reveal that a segment of society harbors some plainly irrational fear of the agency's program. It might be possible for the administrator to remove or reduce this fear, and even if it isn't, the administrator should still know it exists so that he or she will not be caught off guard if and when it explodes. Along with the good news, a prudent administrator will want to hear all the bad news too, simply because it is politically safer than remaining in ignorance.

Properly understood and employed by administrators, public participation in government might occur earlier, more often, and more extensively. It might explore areas of government activity hitherto considered sacrosanct by administrators, such as scientific research and development, economic planning and analysis, and technical innovation. Citizen participation will not contaminate these activities; it might grant them a new measure of social utility, to say nothing of political legitimacy.

Public administrators now holding citizen participation in fear and loathing ought to reconsider their veiw of it. If they do, they just might embrace it for the reasons I have outlined here. It's been said lately that public administrators don't seem to be doing such a hot job. One reason they appear to be failing is that, in reality, they don't possess the authority they need to fulfill their responsibilities. As many presidential appointees have learned, the power given them in their certificate of appointment is not worth the paper it is written on. Since, as I have observed, they are not all fools or crooks, the smart and responsible ones might do well to extend their hands in friendship and cooperation to the public waiting at their door, demanding to be admitted to the process of administration. They will not be weakened if they do, but strengthened.

We Are All Scientists Now

Science has penetrated our lives so pervasively that we have little choice but to come to terms with it. I believe this can be done and that the tensions and conflicts between citizens and science can be reconciled. The first step is this: Scientists must come down off their pedestals and accept the intellectual validity of public participation in science policy.

Those of us advocating greater participation have invoked moral, ethical, and legal reasons until we have grown hoarse. It is time to look at the substantive contributions citizens make to scientific decisions. On those grounds, I think we can persuade scientists that it is unscientific to ignore them. People do know things that are worth knowing, even to science.

It is literally impossible for scientists working alone to discern all the impacts of a new technology. They cannot predict its social and environmental impacts, but should they work in ignorance of them? Might not their work be improved if it were informed of these consequences? Public participation is a way of flagging these problems in advance. The untrained eye of the ordinary citizen might just catch some obvious shortcoming that the trained eye has missed. Reality has an infinite number of dimensions and science cannot be expected to take them all into account.

Citizens are usually the first to detect the unintended consequences of technology, if only because they get sick or die from the effects or because their physical surroundings are harmed. But we should not depend upon tragedy to inform us when citizens are everyday assessing technologies with their eyes ("it's ugly"), their ears ("it's noisy"), their noses ("it stinks"), and their common sense and intuition ("this doesn't make sense").

While scientists can perform dazzling feats if they are provided a social vacuum in which to work, social problems are rarely amenable to purely technical solutions. Strangely enough, it has been fashionable these last few years to declare that, if Americans can put a man on the moon, then we can abolish war or end poverty or eliminate crime. But putting men on the moon is _easy_ compared with solving social problems.

Science policy involves the public use of science to address social problems. But to address social problems requires social data. It's important to know what people think and feel, what they hope and fear, what they expect, even when they are being unreasonable. The methods of science have a vital, but small place in securing this data.

Scientific methods were not, are not, and cannot be intended as a substitute for direct public participation. People are not a mass of raw material waiting for some scientist to come along and mine. Instead of studying the people, let the people speak for themselves. Let them contribute their data directly.

Public participation is also a good way to tap society for new sources of technical and social innovation. Industrial science often assumes that people are all alike. It then acts upon this assumption by deploying homogenizing technologies throughout society, such as fast food, television, and automobiles.

Yet America is still a land teeming with natural and cultural diversity. Science should serve and reinforce this diversity instead of trampling it underfoot. If science did there would be boundless opportunity for technological innovation. Energy technologies in the Great Plains (windpower) could differ from energy technologies used in coastal areas (harnessing tides). Food technologies in cities (roof-top gardens) might differ from those in the suburbs (common gardens). Shelter technologies in the Southwest (adobe) might differ from those in New England (stone). Transportation technologies for the young (bicycles) might differ from those for the elderly (electric carts). But industrial science ignores these diverse options because it is easier and more profitable for large-scale technologies to turn out products on a massive assembly-line basis.

Science should recognize that voluntary citizen organizations are already producing research of high quality. The Council on

Economic Priorities, for example, a public interest research organization in New York City, has won acclaim for its rigorous but innovative analyses of corporate performance in such areas as pollution control and minority employment. They survive economically by selling their reports to businesses and these reports sell like hot cakes because they are so good. Such organizations produce excellent research because industrial science has failed to do so. Three decades of fat federal subsidies for research and development have deadened some of the critical faculties of technological enterprise in America. Scientists are too busy addressing the questions they are paid to address to notice that a number of other questions are going begging. Sometimes the questions going unattended are the most important questions. Sooner or later, they fall into the laps of citizen organizations who take on the job of researching them.

Groups such as the Environmental Defense Fund and the Natural Resources Defense Council, which combine litigation with research, are leaders in citizen-based environmental research, but they are not alone. Citizens fighting highways threatening their neighborhoods have been forced to research alternative community transportation options that official planning agencies and their consulting firm contractors have neglected. Citizens fighting power plants have been forced to develop alternate regional energy plans. Citizens fighting redlining of their neighborhoods have been forced to design alternate community economic development schemes.

These citizen research projects are usually produced with assistance from dissidents and mavericks in the professions whose contributions are *pro bono publico*. Their reports, though humble in appearance and produced at low cost, are often clearer, more honest, and more technically sound than the inpenetrable volumes routinely disgorged by official planning agencies.

This research and the new model of cooperation between science and citizens represented by this research offers, it seems to me, hope for science at large. If scientists can stop denigrating this new form of research and begin to examine its validity, they might be pleasantly surprised. It may be a way of resolving the debate in the scientific community over whether science can or should address social values. This debate is an intense one and it must be resolved sooner or later. Values won't go away and neither will science. And the war between them is harming us all.

Public participation is the best method we have for addressing the social values implicit in science policy. Countless voluntary groups have been formed to assert one or another social value. Consulting them on a systematic basis is a way at least to start returning science to its role as a trusted servant of society.

Consider the cobbler. A cobbler does many good things when he repairs a shoe. His work conserves energy and material. He doesn't pollute the environment. He runs a small business that pays taxes and reinforces the local economy. He may hire a helper or two, thus creating employment for others. Though he doesn't grow rich or famous, the cobbler is quite a citizen. I think he deserves a medal or maybe even an honorary Ph.D. Enterprise on this scale is a key to the future, just as it was to much past success.

My friend, the late E. F. Schumacher, author of Small Is Beautiful: Economics As If People Mattered, loved to surpirse people by telling them he was one generation removed from a pig farmer. "What do you mean?" they would exclaim. "Your father was a famous economist in Germany!" As indeed he was. "No, I mean my eldest son," Schumacher would say. "*He* is a pig farmer." In Schumacher's view, being a pig farmer represented a step up from academic intellectualism. He was proud of his son for doing the appropriate thing in his circumstances. Pigs are somehow more real than academic treatises, and conditions now compel us to return to reality on the scale of the pig.

Social change in America and elsewhere got a tremendous boost from Schumacher's book. When I read it, I felt scales fall from my eyes and a whole new world view swam into place before me. Here was a philosophy that addressed in practical fashion the central dilemma of our time: How can we pursue economic well-being in a manner consistent with social justice and ecological stability? Schumacher, tapping the rich view of decentralist thought that runs throughout history and includes the work of such figures as Tolstoy and Gandhi, provided us with a fresh synthesis. He reconceptualized our problems and proposed a brand new set of potential solutions. He did this by creating a new metaphysical basis for economics.

We environmentalists knew in our guts that ecological protection simply could not be on an inevitable collision course with social and economic justice, although that charge was constantly hurled at us. For instance, we were continually told that society could not "afford" clean air. We were told that efforts to reduce pollution would destroy jobs and deprive poor people of economic opportunity. Conventional wisdom ordained that only capital investment in industry would promote employment. But Schumacher made us see that, in fact, capital investment by corporations is largely used to purchase complex technologies that reduce employment, and thereby labor costs, in order to create profits.

Typically, labor constitutes the largest portion of the cost of industrial production. The name of the game is to reduce costs and to increase profits. To reduce costs, you reduce employment. Machines may be expensive initially, but once you have paid for them, you are home free, for machines are cheaper than human labor and they don't go on strike. (However, they do break down and malfunction, but traditional economics pays scant attention to this shortcoming.) Naturally, the yardstick used by business to measure success is not how many jobs are generated, even though society as a whole has a great interest in generating more, not less, employment. By its standard, big business is succeeding because it is making money. While I do not quarrel with the right of big business to make money, I wonder if it can't be done while increasing, not lowering, levels of employment.

If a basic thrust of business is to reduce levels of employment, then who is to provide it? The government? I saw a news special on television not long ago about the problem of unemployment in Mexico that concluded that the Mexican government would have to produce forty million new jobs over the next decade. This conclusion struck me as ludicrous. In my bemusement, I wondered if any soul alive on the planet today really believes that the government of Mexico is capable of producing forty million new jobs over the next decade? Mind you, I don't hold the government of Mexico in any particular disregard. I extend to it the same skeptical attitude I feel for all centralized authority. I doubt the capability of government anywhere to produce many millions of new jobs, particularly given present and growing constraints in energy, capital, and resources.

Forty million new jobs! It boggles the mind. It's time to consider the advice of E. F. Schumacher:

If things become so vast that the mind cannot any more "encompass" them, a sense of proportion becomes an impossibility. When we are told that there are, say, 8 million unemployed in the United States, the size of the problem paralyzes our imagination and all we can do is have nightmares. It would be different if we were told that there are, for example, 90 unemployed in our neighborhood. We could then focus on the problem, find out who they are, what they could do, what they would want to do. Local action would then become at least conceivable: it is not even conceivable as long as our minds are fixed on large national totals.

Schumacher's way of making complicated problems clear and simple appealed to me and, or course, to many thousands of others. However, most people assume that complicated problems require complicated answers. A friend of mine, a leading citizen activist in California, heard of Schumacher through me and caught him on a Los Angeles television interview program where he was asked, "What would you do to solve the state's problems if you were the governor?" Schumacher answered, "Why I don't know. I haven't a clue." With some exasperation, my friend called me to report this and to ask, "Why are you out touting this guy? He doesn't know anything! He said so himself!" I responded, "You are missing the point. Schumacher's answer is the only right one. California is too big! That's the problem! By frankly confessing his inability to solve California's problems, Schumacher was trying to get you to focus on the problem of scale. It is refreshing to have someone admit that nothing can be done so long as things are too big and complicated. If only our politicians would do this, we'd be a lot better off."

Schumacher's willingness to play the fool, so to speak, in order to make his point was one of the many charming attributes he possessed. This quality never deserted him. Early in 1977, shortly after Jimmy Carter had become president, Schumacher was in Washington, D. C., and a meeting between him and the new president was arranged. A serious-minded Jimmy Carter greeted Schumacher in the Oval Office and they sat down to talk. The president knew that a lot of people, including California Governor Jerry Brown, regarded Schumacher as a new economic guru and so, expecting a complicated answer, he asked him, "Dr. Schumacher, what advice can you give me about fighting rising inflation and unemployment?" "I think you should plant trees," said Schumacher. The president blinked. "What did you say?" he asked. "Plant more trees," repeated Schumacher amicably. The president blinked again. Was this guy off his rocker?

Once again, Schumacher was giving the best answer. When the complicated answers fail to work, as they have, why not try the simple ones? He had recently written a lovely eassy on trees and all the good things that they do. Trees provide shade and cooling from the heat of the sun. They collect and store solar energy and use it to produce such good things to eat as fruit and nuts. They are a renewable resource; they can be cut down to provide wood that can be used to warm us or to build shelters for ourselves. Trees are machines for photosynthesis and thus supply us with the oxygen we need to breathe. They enrich the soil. They beautify the world. Obviously, these are important functions and we would be hard pressed to survive without them. Yet, all around the world, we are cutting down trees as fast as we can. The Amazon basin, the last great tropical forest left to the planet, is shrinkly daily thanks to development pressures. The lungs of the planet are going!

The functions of trees in providing us with food, energy, housing, employment, and a livable environment is something presidents should understand. Better they should see this transcendent simplicity than be blinded by elaborate, arcane, and ultimately meaningless policy processes. Schumacher was right to tell Jimmy Carter to plant more trees, and Jimmy Carter would have been smart to take his advice.

Schumacher's assertion that scale is the primary problem applies to both capitalist and socialist countries. He observed that both the United States and Russia have fallen under the rule of mammoth bureaucracies committed only to their self-perpetuation and to hopeless notions of unending economic growth, based on exploitation of dwindling natural resources and blind faith in increasing technological complexity.

Economics is flawed in basic ways, Schumacher taught. According to him, economics assumes that labor is a bad thing, and onerous drudgery is to be minimized if not eliminated altogether. Understandably, and forgivably, such early economists as Adam Smith were motivated by the vision of human liberation through economic development: End hard labor so that people could be free to grow and develop in all the wonderful ways available to them. What inspired the founders of economics was not greed, but the laudable dream of a better life for all, a life in which the anxiety of material insecurity would be banished permanently through the prowess of technology. Let machines do the work! Tap the abundant resources of the earth and put them to work for the people too! This powerful vision carried the day; in fact, it succeeded all too well.

Once humans get something going, they don't know how to stop it. A thick crust of self-interest builds up around it that is virtually impenetrable. Our flight from material insecurity and from the drudgery of labor has landed us in an industrial prison into which no light of spiritual yearning is allowed. Look, says Schumacher, work is not inherently bad. People are born to do some kind of work; it is a basic form of self-expression. We cannot escape from our obligation to work. As a moral proposition, we <u>ought</u> to provide for our own basic needs. We ignore this obligation at our risk, whether we expect another person or a machine to do our work for us. But work should be creative and satisfying, not degrading drudgery. (Some drudgery, however, <u>is</u> inescapable; babies' diapers must be changed and no machine can do it. So who is to do this unpleasant task and on what terms?) But work should and can be creative and satisfying, not degrading drudgery. We must look anew at what sort of work we do, why we do it, and how we organize it. Maybe we can reduce the drudgery to a minimum or distribute it more evenly. If all the absolutely necessary drudgery in the world were redistributed fairly among us, maybe each of us would have to spend only a few hours a week taking care of it. Such a scheme might even provide a pleasant change of pace. It's visionary, I know, but would this arrangement be so bad?

Along with its bias against labor, at the root of the economic vision that animates both capitalist and socialist societies lie two other fundamental biases, one that favors technology and another that favors the exploitation of natural resources. Thus workers' fears that they will be replaced by machines turn out not to be irrational but the logical, inexorable outcome of assumptions hidden within the supposedly objective science of economics. Similarly, the fears of environmentalists that economic analysis will inevitably lead to greater exploitation of natural resources are well founded. Most economists refuse to admit that they are trained to incorporate these assumptions into their professional analyses. But this is how they continually reach such conclusions as society's inability to "afford" clean air. They consistently fail to add up all the economic damage done by air pollution, and they fail entirely to address its social costs, such as damages to public health or aesthetic values.

The flight from human labor to production by machines was intended, again, to increase and ensure material security; but in some ways it has threatened our security by making us vulnerable to the weaknesses inherent in large systems remote from community control.

Agricultural societies, no doubt, had their drawbacks; but except in times of unusual conditions most people could feed themselves with food products of their own or of the surrounding community. Today that is no longer true. Monocultural food production by large agribusiness operations is growing vulnerable to assault by whatever natural predators feed upon the crop being raised. Pesticide experts have trouble staying one step ahead of these predators since they keep adapting to whatever pesticides are used to eliminate them. And of course the massive use of pesticides themselves adds to the overall vulnerability of the food system by concentrating toxic substances in soil, water, and the very food crops the pesticides are intended to protect. Moreover, pesticides are derived from increasingly expensive chemicals, largely petroleum based, and this system too is wobbly. No matter how much additional capital or technology we deploy, we may have exhausted their possibilities. Once again, the imperatives of industrialization—centralization, complexity, conformity—have led us into danger.

Schumacher urges us to go the other way, to create thousands of new small work places that apply many small- or intermediate-scale technologies. "If you give a hungry man a fish," says Schumacher, "you have done him a favor; but it you equip him to fish for himself, you have done him a much greater one." He demonstrates the relationship between labor-intensive activities (those that rely primarily on physical exertion rather than primarily on costly, complex, and large-scale machinery) and the stability of democratic institutions. Simply put, the more people themselves supply their own material needs, the less subject they are to manipulation and exploitation by others.

Moreover, Schumacher asserts that the job-creating and human-liberating qualities of small- and intermediate-scale technologies are equaled by their tendency to conserve energy and to minimize environmental damage. People working with their hands say, on a community garden or greenhouse, or a "sweat equity" project wherein the human labor and energy used to restore neighborhood housing is that of the people who will live there, use less energy and do less harm to the environment than do such complicated tools as nuclear power plants. Schumacher's assertion that labor-intensive activities tend to be environmentally benign offers a new basis, by the way, for close collaboration between environmentalists and labor unions, two powerful public constituencies that are now too easily and too often divided by assertions that providing clean air and clean water means the loss of jobs.

Schumacher believed that sensitive design of new tools, keyed to the precise ecological and cultural setting where they are to be used, would result in what he calls "appropriate technology," that is, technology uniquely suited to the social niche it is to occupy. Appropriate technologies are made from materials available locally, and their manufacture and use are adapted to the skills and knowledge of local inhabitants. They should be relatively inexpensive and easy to use and maintain, thus reducing reliance upon remote and vulnerable sources of supply or specialized skills. By appropriate technology, Schumacher meant to address <u>the scale</u> of the needed technology. By and large, what we need now are technologies somewhat larger and more complex than a hoe or a kettle, but significantly smaller and less complex than a nuclear power plant.

Economic activities that employ appropriate technologies to create jobs conserve energy, and protect the environment are not utopian schemes. In fact, some existing government programs already fill the bill. The President's Council on Environmental Quality once assembled a sort of "small is beautiful" public works program drawn from legally authorized federal activities. The purpose of this exercise was to recommend measures that might combat inflation and unemployment simultaneously while enhancing or at least not disturbing the environment. Among the government programs that the council judged as fitting these criteria were erosion control; reclamation and fencing on public lands; reforestation; upgrading of historic houses and districts; insulating housing, which provides jobs for construction workers, keeps people warmer, and conserves energy; highway repair and maintenance; and railroad roadbed repair and development.

These programs can be potent tools in the fight against economic "stagflation" simply because they can be started quickly and their economic benefits felt quickly. They do not require long-term planning, nor do they depend upon complex, capital-intensive machinery in order to work. These programs do depend upon human labor, including ample demand for low skills, a resource in abundant supply. People without technical training need to eat, too; they need jobs.

Also inherent in the concept of appropriate technology is boundless new opportunity for small business. Schumacher's call for the creation of thousands of new work places is a call for the revival of small-scale capitalism. Because appropriate technologies tend to be easy to manage and maintain, they are well suited for use by small groups and communities.

Certainly existing appropriate technologies evolved chiefly from small-scale enterprises, such as the New Alchemy Institute in Woods Hole, Massachusetts. This alternative technology project founded by former antiwar activists designs and tests environmentally benign human support systems. Their work with aquaculture, agriculture, wind systems, and solar technology is on a scale accessible to families and small businesses. Virtually all current experimentation and innovation in appropriate technology is being done by small entrepreneurs, often under harsh conditions and without benefit of public or corporate subsidies or other conventional support. Until recently, established social institutions—government, business, universities, the professions—have been either indifferent to or contemptuous of appropriate technology. As pointed out earlier in these essays, large institutions appear incapable of thinking about small-scale endeavors, let alone providing them for society. These institutions appear incapable of the refined social analysis that must of necessity accompany the design and introduction of small- and intermediate-scale technology. But if the needs that gave rise to the idea of appropriate technologies—economic decentralization, labor-intensity, energy and environmental conservation, and local self-reliance—are genuine, then there exists a vast market for technologies. It may be that small business, which is otherwise locked in a losing battle with "bigness," is uniquely equipped to meet the new challenge of "smallness."

What E. F. Schumacher achieved in his famous little book was a clear and simple definition of the key debate before us in this decade of the eighties. Is big better? Is small beautiful? By convincing a lot of people to focus on scale as a primary problem, he reduced the massive confusion surrounding our public dialogue. By reconceptualizing the problems besetting us, he showed us how we could serve the needs of workers, the poor, and small business without sacrificing the natural environment. He taught us to appreciate the wisdom and validity of small-scale enterprise for small good things add up.

I am reminded of one of my favorite examples of appropriate technology, a mental-health halfway house in Massachusettts where some of the residents designed and constructed a solar greenhouse. A number of good things flowed from this project. The greenhouse was used to raise vegetables that were consumed by the residents, thereby improving their nutrition and lowering their food costs. The greenhouse was also used to raise flowers that the residents sold in a local marketplace, thereby earning some money. But best of all, the people involved in the greenhouse project got better! The horticultural therapy worked. Since then a couple of the residents of this halfway house have created jobs for themselves in helping people at similar residences build their own solar greenhouses. This is a small success story, I know, but how many institutions of this type are there across the country that could benefit from solar greenhouses? How much food could be produced? How much energy conserved? How much employment generated? And how many people given a meaningful interest?

Had he lived long enough to hear of this example, Schumacher would have loved it just as he loved all the evidence that people and communities all over the world are reassuming a measure of control over their futures. He was optimistic because he was convinced that we possess unlimited talent and ingenuity for devising tools to serve our real needs. Yes, some critics tried to dismiss him as anti-technology, anti-growth, or anti-development, but to the contrary, he gave technology a new lease on life and imbued economics with a new theoretical basis. Science and economics, Schumacher taught, should not be allowed to forget that they are servants of humanity's chief, but humble, goal of decent survival.

Small Is Inevitable

Nearly everyone aware of current events knows that the planet has a limited and diminishing supply of fossil fuels. Sure, some reserves remain, but they tend to be in hard-to-reach places, like under the North Sea, and tapping them is very difficult and costly, which is yet another reason for soaring energy costs. All the easily obtainable supplies of oil and coal have already been exploited and getting at the remainder will take a lot of energy. So we will have to put in more to get out less. This is a limit to growth, a physical one.

Conceptual limits to growth exist too. They are just as real as physical ones, but they are harder to see. For example, if we increased the number of scientists in society by a hundred times, would we get a hundred times more knowledge or a hundred times better technology? The answer is probably no. When science was young and vigorous, it discovered a lot of things we needed to know, like how to vaccinate people against smallpox. This was all to the good, but by now, science seems to have discovered most easily discoverable knowledge, just as the energy companies have exploited the most accessible supplies of fossil fuels. Fewer and fewer quick fixes are likely to result from increased investments in scientific research; this field has been overtilled. This doesn't mean that there are limits to knowledge or discovery (there aren't) but that industrialized science, with its commitment to big, easy, central solutions, has run its course. From here on out, the going is harder.

Institutional limits to growth are another factor. Central authority cannot make us all happy or secure, that is clear. But can central authority even continue to send out Social Security checks? There is, I suppose, a time to centralize and a time to decentralize. Had I been alive in 1933, no doubt I would have been an ardent advocate of the New Deal. I would have cheered the appearance of each new alphabet agency as if it were an angel of heaven. In those days, New Deal agencies were small and new, and hence more vigorous in addressing abuses of the industrial order. But those days have past. Now is a time to decentralize. We have no way to go but small.

Plenty of advantages await us along this new path. Other forms of resources may be declining, but there is still no limit to human energy, talent, skill, and ingenuity. All over America, people are standing around doing nothing because they do not have a "job." They are bored, frustrated, insecure, and surely tired of waiting for somebody "in charge" to tell them what to do. But there are plenty of things for them to do. They don't need a degree in nuclear physics to pick up trash, clean streets, plant flowers and vegetable gardens, paint houses, and maintain parks and recreation areas. Millions more have "jobs" that are demeaning and degrading that could be less so if work were designed as if the people doing it mattered.

Reality is doing a lot of instructing. As the industrial economy declines, we need a new recognition of the inherent dignity of labor, a point the economists have purposefully neglected, thereby persuading millions of people that humble work is humiliating work. Gandhi, who made a point of personally cleaning urinals wherever he went, was trying to tell us that this is not so. Let us revise our views about work so that basic, essential needs are not despised, but honored as they should be.

As much as we have abused it, we Americans still possess a terrific knack for science and technology. Call it American know-how or Yankee ingenuity or what you will, but from the Erie Canal on, Americans have not been afraid to tinker with technologies of every kind. We are temperamentally inclined to devise and improve tools, out of this proclivity has grown a technical prowess that has become world renowned. Even at this stage of disenchantment, when a lot of unexpected, unintended adverse consequences are coming home to roost, American science is still probably the single most prestigious force in the world. It is something to fear, to be in awe of, but still something to marvel at. With all its flaws, American science still promises much, though we are much less certain about it than we once were.

Today many of us are disillusioned with science. In a way, it is liberating not to be under the spell that had us so intoxicated for so long. For decades we placed all our bets on science and technology. We took it as an article of faith that bigger was better. Now we know better! The lessons we have learned are invaluable, and we may have learned them just in the nick of time. We now know that, in the context of natural systems, there is no such thing as waste. In nature, everything is used to maximum advantage and we must learn to emulate nature's true efficiency. Human waste, in this view, is not something to be disposed of so much as it is something valuable to be made use of.

Let us be glad that we have come down from our technologically induced high, that we finally have been taught humility about the limits of tools. Work—not capital, not technology—is sacred. Let us consciously choose enobling employment. Big, total solutions to the challenges of producing goods are fantasies we can well be rid of. We have learned that things are part of a whole; to fiddle around with one thing invariably affects another. So we must, of necessity, broaden our perspectives to include the whole. This learning, which has sometimes been painful, can do us much good.

In our confusion and disappointment, we have stumbled upon the keys to the future. We now know that we must be ever conscious of scale. We now know that diversity—both cultural and natural—must be preserved because it is relentlessly functional. We know that local communities and biological regions are intelligible to people whereas the vast, remote abstraction of the nation is not.

We have always possessed the ability to devise technologies that are compatible with social goals. In the past, we were too innocent to see the connections. Now we are being forced to. Let us get on with the task of creating technologies that are quiet, nonpolluting, energy conserving, labor intensive, and easily operated and maintained.

Here are some examples:

- In Cedar County, Nebraska, fifty family farms have joined together to form the Small Farm Energy Project, which is testing low-cost solar technologies such as grain dyers, farrowing barns, and wind-powered electric generators. By working together voluntarily, they are experimenting in ways no one of them alone could afford. These farming families are doing this work not because they are liberals or conservatives or socialists or kooks; they are doing it to preserve family farms.
- The town of Hercules, California, recently constructed an innovative waste-water treatment plant called the Solar Aquacell, a totally enclosed lagoon inside a greenhouse cover that treats wastewater with a biological system using water plants and tiny animals to consume wastes. Because the plant was considered experimental and because the town refused to hook it up to a larger, centralized conventional system, federal and state grants were denied the project. But the town decided they would be better off in the long run with innovative technology. They built and paid for the plant themselves.
- In Chicago, the South Shore National Bank has adopted a policy that all monies deposited there are to be reinvested in the surrounding neighborhood. As a result, much housing has been upgraded and new industry has been attracted to this urban neighborhood. The ultimate goal is to turnover the bank ownership

to citizens in the neighborhood.

- In Cheyenne, Wyoming, senior citizens and teenagers work side by side to produce food for themselves, for local "meals on wheels" programs, and for sale to the public. They are working in America's largest solar greenhouse. The structure was designed and built by volunteers and it is now largely staffed by volunteers. The project is four years old and continues to expand food production.

We should delve into all kinds of mixtures of scale. What is big anyway? A simple technology like smallpox immunization can be performed on a global scale, even by local volunteers, as it was. Simple technologies can be and ought to be widely replicated; complex technologies cannot be established in more than a few places since they demand an inevitable, dangerous degree of centralization.

Complex technologies on a small scale, however, may apply to and operate in one place only. That, too, is fine. William Ellis, an appropriate technologist in Maine, once tried to secure a grant from the National Science Foundation on behalf of the Maine lobster industry. He believed that new small-scale technologies, specially designed and fitted to this particular niche, could save the industry from going under. The people at NSF studied the proposal and concluded that it was good, but they declined to fund it because, as they said, even if it worked it could only benefit the Maine lobster industry. Their criteria demanded that grants be made only for proposals with national applicability. Let the lobster industry in Maine sink, it does not fit national standards. The patriotic cry ought to be: Remember the Maine lobster industry!

If small is inevitable, what signs indicate that this is so? The signs are all around us and grow more evident with each day that passes. Social movements are the true agents of social change, movements dedicated to decentralization and diversity are springing up all over the country. There are citizen movements on behalf of ethnic groups, neighborhoods, family farms, small towns, health food, community gardens, human potential, physical fitness, and sexual diversity. Social change may be an untidy garden; it does not meet laboratory standards of sterile purity. But it is blooming vigorously all the same.

Meanwhile, countless technological innovations are popping up in the areas of alternative energy, alternative food production, alternative education, and alternative health care. The countereconomy is a multibillion-dollar business. It is also producing lots of jobs for people who didn't formerly fit into the conventional employment pigeonholes and who thought dropping out was the only alternative. These same people are now sitting on local school boards, county commissions, and the boards of consumer cooperatives. Dropping out has become dropping in!

Somehow these myriad experiments fit together. They interconnect, reinforcing and complementing one another. A basic set of new values is at play here: cooperation, community, equality, diversity, and ecology are the bywords. These value shifts are being nudged along not only by talented, dedicated people but by the times and by nature itself. What an irresistible combination!

Why are all these heartening developments little known to the world at large? One reason is that they originate primarily in voluntary efforts that don't show up on that big neon sign called the Gross National Product. If citizens band together to build a solar collector for a community center, the factotums of economics sitting in think tanks or government agencies don't hear about it; therefore, they can't count it. If they can't count it, it doesn't exist. So they say it can't be done and, if tried, it won't work. But we shouldn't worry too much about such faulty measuring systems. What cannot be counted, cannot be controlled. So much the better for freedom.

Small is inevitable. The human race is not about to depart from life's stage without putting up a good fight. The force of life is at least as strong as the force of death and destruction. A rough justice exists out there somewhere in the universe. It will not let us down. Our prospects may be nip and tuck. But come to think of it, life offers us pretty good odds.

Accountability Is Power

In large part, people pay taxes, serve in armies, and otherwise obey the law not because they are forced to, but becaue they have been taught from birth to revere some supreme source of authority. Force alone, however great, can never secure this degree of social consent, at least not over the long haul. Thus, to survive and to function, social institutions must maintain a strong measure of moral legitimacy that approaches, if it does not always reach, sacredness. If you are thinking this is a big order to fill, you are right.

In most times and places, the source of authority the conveyer of legitimacy, is taken to be the people themselves. True, most rulers down through history have been unwilling to pay more than lip service to this concept, but few rulers have been allowed to openly deny it for long. "The principle of the sovereignty of the people, which is always to be found, more or less, at the bottom of almost all human institutions, generally remains there concealed from view," said Alexis de Tocqueville in Democracy in America. "It is obeyed without being recognized, or if for a moment it be brought to light, it is hastily cast back into the gloom of the sanctuary." So it is that monarchs claiming to rule by divine right (by the way, most of the European thrones were originally elective ones) have long disappeared from the face of the earth. And even the fiercest dictators feel compelled to prop up their regimes from time to time with sham elections and referenda.

The principle of the sovereignity of the people got a big boost from the American Revolution. The founders installed the will of the people as the direct source of authority unencumbered by crown or church. They consciously designed a system of government to maximize the accountability of social institutions to the people at large (without overdoing it to the point of chaos or irresponsibility). The framers of the Constitution earnestly believed that the people (admittedly, at the beginning, consisting only of property-owning white males), exercising democratic processes within democratic institutions, would govern more wisely than all the kings and bishops put together.

Somewhere along the way, things went haywire. In the vast technical and economic regulatory bureaucracies where most of the real power of government now fretfully reposes, the people, far from comprising society's ultimate source of authority, are actually perceived as a contemptible herd to be shoved this way and that for their own good. Technocrats may not agree on much else, but they are firm in their agreement that ordinary citizens have no direct place in the operations of government. The idea of government by the scientific method has greatly eroded the concept of citizen control. Analysis is exalted over synthesis, quantification over common sense, efficiency over politics, and technology over morality. Simultaneously, the industrial complexes have further weakened citizen control by assuming a supra-Constitutional economic power beyond the reach of democratic processes. As if this weren't a sufficient assault on the spirit and letter of the Constitution, we endured during the era of the Vietnam War and Watergate an abuse of authority without parallel in American history.

A major thrust of industrialism, and hence of recent political and economic history, has been a flight from accountability. Industrial managers fled from stockholders, workers, and consumers rather than account to them for their actions and plans. Accountability is viewed with distaste and as a form of weakness by the forces of industrialism. Besides, accountability is tedious, difficult, and time-consuming; it is inefficient and uneconomic. In much the same way and for much the same reasons, public administrators have also fled from accountability. Neither the president nor the Congress can really get on top of technical bureaucracies because, if nothing else, the bureaucracies have so many good ways of evading accountability; here lies, at last, their true expertise.

Actually, two basically different concepts of power should

be examined here. One concept of power is the macho image: power as destructive force; power as cold, demanding, inflexible authority; power as tough, sure, confident, aggressive, arrogant, intimidating leadership; power as the ability to grant or withhold special privileges and material rewards. This image of power admits no accountability to anyone or anything, except possibly to some abstract notion of God and country or destiny. This conception of power is all too real. Genghis Kahn, sweeping across Eurasia bringing death and destruction to all who would not immediately submit to his total authority, is one example of it.

The second basic concept of power is the creative image: power as the ability to help others; power as flexibility and receptivity; power as shared enthusiasm and commitment; power as the moral and honorable exercise of authority within a set of ground rules to which the people as a whole have agreed. This is power constrained and enabled by accountability. Citizen networks, for example, create and exercise power in a way that runs directly counter to the macho conception. In a network setting, you are never able to act without regard to the wishes of other people in the network. But in this setting, accountability _is_ power! It is the course of power and the instrument of it. If a networker decides to move in a certain direction, and he or she has done a good job of networking—that is a careful, sensitive prearrangement and sharing of data—then when the networker moves, the network moves too. In this way a lot of people quietly assume a new tactic, a new opinion, or a new program and begin to promote it through their own networks. If this isn't power, I don't know what is.

Hazel Henderson frequently makes the point that we have at last entered an age wherein morality is pragmatic, that is, if the species is to survive, we are going to _have_ to treat each other better. My corollary to this is that we have entered a political climate in which accountability is power, that is, if social institutions are to survive and reacquire moral legitimacy, they are going to have to reinvite citizen control and public participation.

We must remember that the only power we ever consented to was power constrained by accountability. Any other form of power is illegitimate and immoral, and if our colleges and universities have turned out a couple of generations of technocrats who are oblivious to the requirements of accountability, then the citizenry must take the reins of power from them and climb into the driver's seat. Power constrained by accountability can do many things that destructive power cannot. It can restore social consent and thereby consensus. It can renew mandates for social institutions and restore dignity to public office. It can reorder national priorities.

Now that a conservative political revolution has occurred, we find ourselves needing the healing application of accountability to the exercise of power more than ever. We almost have to reinvent it to suit the unique conditions we face. Several years ago when I helped organize the successful fight to stop the American supersonic transport (SST), I learned a simple, powerful lesson: It makes no difference whether a member of Congress is liberal or conservative, a Democrat or a Republican; if you can generate enough authentic grassroots pressure from the home district or state, that member has to listen. And sometimes—often, as we found with the SST—he or she can be persuaded to vote our way. For instance, the Democratic Senator Clinton Anderson, considered by many to be the father of the aerospace industrial complex, voted against the SST because, he said, on the morning of the vote he received eighty telegrams from his constituency in New Mexico urging him to oppose the SST and that eighty telegrams from New Mexico are a lot.

We have to rebuild accountability in the system from the ground up. The only sensible action for us now is to pick up the cudgels and return to the hard, basic work of community organizing.

The constituencies for social change--minorities, feminists, environmentalists, the counterculture, and others--have been dealt a hard blow by the present conservative trend, but the election has not destroyed them. The potential for a winning coalition is still present and I firmly believe that social change groups are the only ones who really have a practical program for guiding the country into a stable postindustrial future.

The conservatives don't know that we are experiencing the decline of industrialism as we have known it, an historic process that cannot be halted or reversed. All the king's horses and all the king's men cannot put Detroit back together again. My advice: Hang onto your hats and organize, organize, organize!

It's never been harder. When Richard Nixon was in power, we had a Democratic Congress to act as a buffer. And public interest groups were in their heyday, bringing litigation and doing research to counter corporate and bureaucratic abuses. Public interest advocacy must, of course, continue, but community organizing has to be the top priority.

Without an authentic, discernible grassroots constituency, public interest lobbying doesn't have the moral legitimacy it needs to obtain respect or to exercise power, and we can be dismissed, with some justification, as tiny bands of extremists or impractical dreamers.

Unfortunately, some public interest groups in the seventies became so absorbed in legal, legislative, and technical issues and processes that they themselves neglected the principle of accountability. Clearly, it is inconsistent, to say the least, for anyone to demand that bureaucracies and corporations practice accountability when the individual or group making this demand is evading it. Now that these legal, legislative, and technical processes are being turned against us, we can find solace and strength in this truest of principles. Our present dilemma is whether we should redouble present levels of public interest litigation, lobbying, and research, or whether we should mobilize a massive grassroots organizing campaign. Or course, it cannot, should not, and will not be all one thing or the other, but I fear we will unthinkingly continue to neglect basic community organizing.

Given the current political climate, we can't afford to do that. Instead we must surface with a fresh mandate or face being treated with disdain and contempt by both the press and the politicians. With this strong new mandate from the grassroots, we will be listened to. If we have to organize bake sales to do it, let's organize bake sales. When we have organized enough of them, we will have revitalized a social movement that even President Reagan and the conservative Congress will have to respect and sometimes defer to.

We can't place our hopes in simply reelecting more liberals to Congress. That may not even be in the cards. Besides, given a choice, it is always better to retain power yourself than to hand it over to someone else, even a well-meaning politician. A community power base can influence and pressure whomever is elected to office. And politicians of every stripe will listen to a strong, well-organized constituency unless he or she is committed to political hari kiri. Efforts to restore liberals to power simply do not possess the same chance for success as community organizing. Liberalism has been discredited, in part, because liberal politicians were so hooked on centralization. They wanted, sincerely, to use central authority to achieve their vision of society. They blew it and while I hate to see them go, having been a liberal myself once upon a time, in some ways they deserve the opprobrium they have fallen into. Now here we are with the conservatives who are as hooked on centralization as the liberals were. The only difference is that they want to use central authority to achieve their vision of restored economic and military might. They will blow it too, given enough time.

What we need is a new vision, generated by all the energy and talent at the grassroots of American society. To achieve this vision, we must not forget the magic secret, which is simple accountability. Public interest groups, most of all, must bear it in mind. Some of them have been altogether too willing to invoke a social movement as the source of their legitimacy, but have been unwilling to account to that movement for their actions. But people at the grassroots are not faceless troops to whom orders are passed down the line. They are flesh and blood human beings with ideas and talents of their own. They are, or should be, full partners in planning goals, policies, tactics, and strategies.

In every American community can be found an indigenous civic leadership that needs to be politically reinforced, psychologically affirmed, and technically assisted. They are the alternative leadership of the country. They are strong, bold, and experienced. They have the guts it takes to be innovators. These people need to be put in touch with others so that they will know they are not working in isolation and so that lessons learned in one place can swiftly be used in others. Organize them! Be organized by them! Account to them and they will account to you. From the power that erupts from this partnership, it is possible to dream again. Human potential remains undiminished, and although even the best of us keep placing obstacles of egotism in our path, the vision of the ideal planetary community, peaceful and just, resting in a beautiful setting of natural abundance and diversity, is as worthy of pursuit as always.

Everything is possible.

Epilogue

One lovely summer's day in 1978, I attended a rally held to oppose construction of a nuclear power plant in Seabrook, New Hampshire. A friendly crowd, rock music, and banners flapping in the breeze created a festive air. In the crowd I spotted many old friends, veterans like me of past campagins for justice, peace, ecology, and other laudable causes. I exchanged warm greetings and fond embraces, hugging someone here and throwing a kiss there. Then I found a seat upon the ground and settled down for what I fully expected to be a ripsnorting good time.

Nothing gets the blood up quite like a rally. Of course, rallies are held to evoke passion and the passion they evoke is exaggerated and intensified by mass experience, which is a strong intoxicant. To feel some powerful emotion—indignation, bliss, rage—in the privacy of your own heart is one thing. To feel it with a crowd is something else. The added wallop can knock you off your feet.

A good rally is really a form of theater in which the crowd is the star. As in the theater, the rally should build to a climax. At this point, everyone in the crowd should be yearning to sacrifice themselves to the cause. Then—pow!—the rally should end, sending the crowd home, sunburned, dusty, exhausted, but committed to a course of action.

At the Seabrook rally, I gazed about happily at the faces (mostly young) in the crowd. On each I could see enthusiasm and determination and I loved them for it. I beamed approvingly as the crowd roared its denunciation of nuclear power, and I listened intently as speaker after speaker, fired by the crowd, climbed new heights of eloquent outrage.

Suddenly, to my surprise, I felt a strange eruption of feeling within me. Before I could blink, I was nearly flattened by it. I managed to retain my outward composure and to fight off an impulse to flee. Something had happened to me.

I wasn't caught up in the mass experience of the rally, I was reacting against it! I no longer felt part of the crowd. Instead, I was viewing it from afar. I felt unutterably sad and almost sick.

What had happened? Had the last remnants of my youth just taken flight? Had I lost my capacity for zeal? Had I suddenly, inexplicably, decided to favor nuclear power? No, thank goodness, none of that! It took me a while, however, to sort out my feelings and to figure out what had happened to me. I had reached a point of knowing too much about the complexity of things. I looked at the crowd and thought, "Oh, my lovely friends, do you have any idea what you are letting yourselves in for? Would you persevere if you did?"

The fight against nuclear power, or any such fight, will test your convictions to the limit. You might as well climb up on the rack, strap yourself in, and instruct the torturers to do their worst. I felt at the Seabrook rally like a parent letting go of a child, knowing just how cold and cruel the world can be and powerless to do anything about it, one way or the other. Maybe I <u>couldn't</u> tell my friends what they were up against. If I tried, would they hear me? Would I only distract them from their urgent work or, even worse, depress them so that their commitment would wane? And maybe I <u>shouldn't</u> try to tell them. They would learn soon enough, in their own good time, in their own way.

Some people must act against social ills, however hard it is to do so. There is no escaping the need for action. "Nobody can become perfect," says the Bhagavad Gita, "by merely ceasing to act." Moreover, we are responsible for our actions and their consequences. Not only must we act, we must choose to act rightly. Slogans may do for a time, but only briefly. Then we must confront the monstrous web of complexity that surrounds all social circumstances and choose with care a course of action that, if we are lucky, will do more good than harm.

Epilogue

The numbing vision of complexity that overtook me at the Seabrook rally was a valid perception. But, I reasoned, I shouldn't allow it to deprive me of my capacity for action. Maybe I should shift gears for awhile and leave the organizing to other younger and more innocent souls; I could write a little book describing what I felt and thought. Compared with the agony that organizing had become for me, I thought that ought to be easy!

It hasn't been easy to write this book. Most organizers I know are great talkers. They could sell refrigerators to Eskimos. Curiously, many organizers can't or don't write. Somehow they need the warm flesh and blood of other people around them all the time in order to work. I am never happier, for example, than when networking face to face or on the phone with a valued collaborator. A typewriter is a poor substitute for this exchange. It doesn't correct you when you are wrong, and it doesn't laugh or cry along with you when that seems the thing to do. So I think I'll get back to the trenches, mud and all. That's where my heart is.

Afterword

It is time that we public interest activists, advocacy researchers, community organizers, and all who lead grassroots movements for social, racial, and sexual equality, economic justice, environmental and consumer protection, and corporate and government accountability, began articulating our personal philosophy. These movements are growing in all mature, industrial societies and are becoming successful. Our ideas, visions, concepts, and ideologies are taking root, showing up in policies, getting coopted by academics and corporations, and being published in "straight" publications (long after we are bored with them). As catalysts of the emerging politics of reconceptualization in industrial societies, we must now take responsibility for ourselves as well as for our programs and visions.

Byron Kennard may be in the vanguard. In this book he philosophizes on his years as an activist in these citizen movements that grew in response to the absurdities of exhausted industrial logic. He cheerfully ransacks society, history, and his own psyche to produce this wise and funny synthesis of his experiences in today's cultural cuckoo's nest. This astringent distillation is the result—one might say, the zen—of social activism.

Byron Kennard is one of the new breed of networkers linking citizens in all industrialized, mass-consumption societies. These informal networks create new information patterns that foster increased local action by autonomous groups sharing similar visions of a sane and humane future for all people on this planet. As Theodore Roszak synthesizes in his book Person/Planet, the needs of the person are now beginning to be perceived as the needs of the planet. Networking makes it possible for local action, informed by planetary awareness, to be orchestrated, not through hierarchy or institutional structure but through sharing.

Since the mid-1960s Byron Kennard and I have jointly "networked" our ideas and actions on many current issues, from combatting environmental pollution and supporting the shift to mass transportation and energy conservation to developing the concepts of public assessment of technology and public interest economics. We have also propagated the ideas of our mutual friend, the late E. F. Schumacher, author of Small Is Beautiful. We shared, too, the dawning understanding of the power of these informal networks in fostering value shifts and social change. At one point, we discussed writing a book together to describe how the processes of networking, social change, and personal actualization seem to flow into larger rivers of value shifts and new cultural expressions. Networking experiences need personal recounting because they are deep and multidimensional, and only the diverse refractions of an individual can adequately reflect this infinitely rich mosaic.

So I am glad that my very dear friend and collaborator has made the time, in the midst of all his tireless organizing activities, to tell his own story in his unique, good-humored, modest style, purposely revealing his own strengths and weaknesses and those of the public interest movement. Byron Kennard knows that we cannot work for constructive social change without self-knowledge. For many headlong activists with messianic visions, this introspection may be too painful. It certainly slows up the revolution and complicates the issues! For this reason, many public interest activists will find this calm voice, eminating from beyond the fire of zealotry, disquieting. But if we are to proceed on the long march toward a saner, more just, and more humane ecological future, we had better back off, reappraise ourselves, and see where we have been.

Yet today many sincerely concerned activists and policy makers see only the proliferating charts portraying all the frightening exponential curves: unrestrained population growth and energy consumption, acceleration in transportation and communication speeds, the turning of arable land into desert, and the rising pollution of air and oceans. All true. But among all these exponential curves, it is easy to miss that there are just as many curves that are cyclic, with gentler rhythms: the ancient patterns of human adaptation and cultural styles.

We need to recognize that human values have always changed with the waxing and waning of cultural styles, that they have always been played out in response to particular resource bases and environments. Byron Kennard also tunes us into history in his special, personal way, making us feel connected to the diurnal drama and rhythmic interplay between destiny and creativity, determinism and free will, chance and necessity. These longer views are healing antidotes to today's linear, Faustian fixations of technological development and economic progress toward secular paradise or escapist space fantasies. He also counters the darker vision of what many see as an inexorable march toward machismo confrontation and Armageddon. All are characteristic world views associated with the maturity and decline of the great wave of culture we have been riding, beginning in fifteenth century Europe with the ideas of Galileo, Copernicus, and Bacon and typified by Rene Descartes's revolt against the unreasoning faith of the medieval church.

Byron Kennard appreciates the fact that, in their time, the ideas of the Enlightenment represented a revolution in values that challenged the devine right of monarchs, mercantilism, feudalism, slavery, and earlier oppressions. Now this 300-year wave of cultural expression is exhausting itself and giving rise to new expressions: the return of the repressed organic, communitarian conviviality and the intuitive "yin" modes of awareness that did not fit the mechanistic, Newtonian, reductionist "yang" styles of the receding eras of the Enlightment and industrialism.

Enfolding these shorter eras is one of the longest cycles of culture, a 3,000-year period that saw the gradual rise of patriarchies and nation states; those highly unstable macromolecules that nucleated around earlier, smaller city states and feudal feifdoms. The exhaustion of the logic of patriarchal nation-states is now painfully apparent. Competition within and between nations, armed confrontation, hierarchical dominance/submission relationships, institutionalized mistrust and machismo technology can only bring destruction in our crowded, interdependent world. Patriarchal policies are ever less credible: hierarchies become bottlenecks; governance by heroic conceptualizers in Washington, Paris, London, Brussels, or Moscow no longer fits any local, real-world situation; and efforts to retool nature with ever more technological fixes only provide a mirror in which emerging systemic thinkers see the urgency of examining ourselves and retooling our values instead. To paraphrase Fritz Schumacher, patriarchal societies now _require_ a breakthrough a day to keep the crises at bay. No wonder the consideration of scale as a separate variable, so evident in Schumacher's _Small Is Beautiful_ and the newly republished _The Breakdown of Nations_ by Leopold Kohr, has become a burning issue!

As patriarchies superseded the earlier matrilineal and matriarchal cultures, they became characterized by their hierarchical structures, centralization, rigid division of labor (and sex roles), and specialization. Another hallmark is the extreme polarization between the conceptual, bureaucratic, academic, intellectual work taking place in centralized, complexes and the intuitive tasks, artistic explorations, and manual work taking place in rural, agricultural, small-town life. The former class of work is rendered operational by the highly aggregated statistical illusions of the formal GNP economy. The unpaid efforts of the nonmonetized "informal economy" of use-value include household production, gardening, canning, repairs, maintenance, nuturing, parenting, and volunteer community service, all cooperative activities that maintain social cohesion and permit the over-rewarded, competitive, "market-place" activities to appear "successful." Thus I heartily agree with Byron Kennard that we must rebalance our individual and social roles and institutions. We must teach our economists to see our economy whole, rather than only the GNP half of it. And we must androgynize our culture and society, rebalancing our collective psyche with a new return of the repressed power and creativity of the yin. We are all prisoners of gender identity, a straightjacket preventing the full flowering of what psychologist Jean Houston calls "the possible human."

Today we see patriarchal leadership becoming even more bizarre. Unconscious of a glaring hypocrisy, these leaders <u>talk</u> a good game, paying lip service to the values of cooperation, peacefulness, humility, and honesty now needed for survival as human numbers have reached the new boundaries of global interdependence. But the patriarchs, whether politicians, corporate executives, or those in academia, labor unions, the churches, or the voluntary sector, are still schizophrenic. They expect to continue placing the heavy burden of making these values operational on the shoulders of subordinated populations: women, minorities, and other "low-caste" groups in their societies. The humbler, more cooperative values do not lend themselves to posturing and machismo heroics; but it is also clear that today industrial cultures cannot tolerate too much more competitive technology and tragic heroics. These cultures now need <u>mothering</u>.

This type of hypocrisy is now least credible and permissible when evidenced by social change and public interest activists, as it was, for example, during the 1960s in the male-dominated antiwar and civil rights movements. Indeed, as Byron Kennard points out, it is in grassroots movements for social justice that such contradictions are the most glaring. Social visionaries and activists, above all, must try to be exemplary emodiments of that which they advocate. Ruefully, Kennard recognizes the egotism and opportunism that sometimes motivate workers for a cause. Similarly, we all recognize the "reformed" patriarchal leaders associated with past policy disasters who "confess," claim to have "recycled themselves," and attempt another chance at bat by coopting the words and slogans of new movements, but never learn the nuances, the spirit, or the music. Thus, many of us who crusaded over the past decade for appropriate technology now curse the day we progagated the phrase, as we see academic grant-hustlers and sanctimonious corporate executives coopting the rhetoric and moving in for fun and profit, in order to accredit the whole field and keep out the riffraff.

Genuine alternatives are as unlikely as ever to emerge from dominant cultures and their elites, since such authentic alternatives always reside repressed in subordinated populations. In the 1960s only the naive would have expected the generals in the Pentagon to get us out of the war in Vietnam. For that deliverance we must thank the young people who protested. In the 1980s the cultural alternatives will not be devised by recipients of grants from the National Science Foundation or from the deliberations of the Domestic Policy Review of Technological Innovation at the White House. The genuine alternatives are alive and growing, as we would expect, on the fringes and and in the interstices of our institutionalized society; in the grassroots, the citizen networks, the media-access activists; from black, Hispanic, Native American, and other ethnic cultures; from the radical feminists, gay peoples' liberation, childrens' liberation, and in the even more radical shift away from anthropocentrism, animal liberation. All of this cultural activity is now putting down economic taproots in what I have called the emerging counter-economy: the organic farm communities; the health food stores and vegetarian restaurants; self-help and holistic health groups; the mutual aid appropriate technology design revolution, with its smaller enterprises and personal, locally based economies; the cooperative and the more convivial communities producing for use-value and human needs; the reciprocity and bartering. It is all there to see, if Washington statisticians could conceptualize it and knew where to point their statistical cameras.

But this bright scenario of emerging renewable-resource technologies, respecting human and nature's rhythms and managed for sustained-yield productivity--while well within our grasp--requires technological innovation less than it does social and cultural innovation and a psychological flowering of human potential, or what Erich Fromm called the revolution from Having to Being. This leap in human consciousness implies full expression of our natural empathy, intuition, creativity, and altruism, and the redefinition of values possible from a larger perspective: that self-interest can and does harmonize with group interest. This is the deeper meaning of Byron Kennard's assertion that everything is possible. We will have redefined the issues and restated the questions. Thus the zen of social activism acknowledges all: the past and what we cannot change, the future, and what we can change--beginning with ourselves. Good social change implies healthy human development; these are two sides of the same coin. It is not enough to organize, educate, and exhort. No longer can we organize only out of sheer animal high spirits or innocence of our own deeper motivations. The liberation movements and healthy self-expression might derail into empty self-assertiveness, and one cannot rally people for long around the banners of narcissism. The ongoing and necessary revolutions against economic injustices are too important to be organized around envy. Confrontations based soley on power leave us too much like our adversaries. We must keep to the higher ground; the moral and value issues that move all great cultural changes.

I must confess that I am no objective commentator on the ideas in this book that Byron Kennard has distilled from his experience. I shared much of the journey with him, as collaborator, coconspirator, co-organizer, and friend. Together we learned that social activism implies the heaviest of responsibilities, since it presumes to redefine the culture and prescribe more desirable alternative futures. So, we cannot get away with merely pointing the way. If we are to be at all believable, we must constantly strive to embody our convictions.

Hazel Henderson

Acknowledgments

Like most authors, I am deeply indebted to others for helping me produce my book. Acknowledging this obligation is a pleasure in every way but one. Unlike most authors, I am a networker and whatever merit inhabits these pages is due in large part to the networking of ideas and actions with others. Exchange of information and insights within the network is a good way to validate them. Frankly, if I thought the views expressed in this book were mine and mine alone, I would shrink from expressing them. I would be too timid. But these views, all of them, have been shared and tested over the years with collaborators whose judgment and character I respect and admire, so I know I can't be too far off the mark. But how do I begin to express gratitude for so long and fruitful a collaboration with so many?

I thought, half seriously, of appending here a directory of my network, but that is virtually impossible and probably undesirable. I myself have stated in these pages that a network is not a directory and can never become one. Networks are far too subtle ever to be captured in print. And that is good. Networks do not cherish exposition, even for the purpose of receiving kudos. Butterflies, presumably, do not wish to be captured and pinned down, whether to be studied or admired. To me, networks are like butterflies: rare, delicate, indescribably beautiful manifestations of life. Social scientists may be eager to analyze them, political opportunists may be eager to exploit them, and corporate foes may be eager to rip off their wings. So why fly into the net if it can be avoided? You will find no directory here. My network will have to make do with this standard postcard greeting:

Dear Network,

How are you? I am fine. Having wonderful time. Wish you were here. See you soon!

Love,

Byron

But even this all-purpose declaration fails to fulfill my obligations. Many friends pitched in generously on this project and I am honor-bound to thank them here by name. Those who provided advice, assistance, and encouragement were Arlene Alligood, Deborah Baldwin, Lee Botts, Tom Chalkley, Joan Claybrook, Sharon Francis, Allison Freeman, Anastasia M. Geanacou, Richard Grossman, Barbara Marx Hubbard, Susan Hufford, Jeffrey Janowitz, Carla Kish, Merle Lefkoff, Mary MacArthur, Michael McCabe, Jeanne Malchon, Sarna Marcus, Ellis Mottur, Wade Rathke, Michael Rawson, Lola Redford, Peter Schuck, John Todd, Lenora Trussell, Congressman Morris L. Udall, Michaela Walsh, and Char White.

Special thanks are due those who made contributions far beyond the calls of duty, of friendship, and even of networking. Ligeia Fontaine edited the manuscript with a loving but careful eye and sent me back to the salt mines of rewrite again and again and I cherish her for it, however much hard labor she put me through. The late Virginia Harbin, a networker if ever there was one, taught me the invaluable lesson that you can perform miracles if you are willing to forego the credit. I could not get through the day without at least one long phone conversation with Peter Harnik, my fellow organizer/networker, who contributed the foreword to this book, but more importantly, has provided me constant assurance that I am not entirely off the wall.

David Hunter, executive director of the Stern Fund, and the Stern Fund itself, has provided much of the financial support for my work over the years and I am deeply grateful to him and to members of the Stern family. They actually provide grants to support social innovation, breaking all the rules of philanthropy.

Mary Ann Massey, who organized with me the citizens' movement for clean air a dozen years ago, is an Irish politician with an unsentimental, no-nonsense approach to government and politics and a former English teacher with a fastidious regard for the language. She has curbed more of my excessive impulses, political and literary, than I care to recall. I have received unflagging encouragement from Glenn David Pinder every step of the way as this book took form and I cannot imagine life without him. One of my first and greatest teachers was Angela Rooney who taught me not only how to fight freeways, but the meaning of citizenship, a high honor and a sacred responsibility.

I also wish to thank Jack D. Howell of Brick House Publishing for inviting me to submit my manuscript when he heard that it was languishing in a dusty box at the back of my clothes closet. All the people at Brick House have my gratitude for bringing out my book when it represented a new departure for them into what might be called the field of political self-reliance. And I am deeply grateful to Linnea Leedham Ochs for the superb job she did of editing the final manuscript.

Lastly, I must mention Hazel Henderson. What she did not teach me, we learned together as we wandered, hand in hand, into places where angels would fear to tread. I thank her for the adventure. I could not have done it without her.